Delphi Quick Syntax Reference

A Pocket Guide to the Delphi and Object Pascal Language

John Kouraklis

Apress®

Delphi Quick Syntax Reference: A Pocket Guide to the Delphi and Object Pascal Language

John Kouraklis
London, UK

ISBN-13 (pbk): 978-1-4842-6111-8   ISBN-13 (electronic): 978-1-4842-6112-5
https://doi.org/10.1007/978-1-4842-6112-5

Managing Director, Apress Media LLC: Welmoed Spahr
Acquisitions Editor: Steve Anglin
Development Editor: Matthew Moodie
Coordinating Editor: Mark Powers

Cover designed by eStudioCalamar

Cover image by Victor Malyushev on Unsplash (www.unsplash.com)

Distributed to the book trade worldwide by Apress Media, LLC, 1 New York Plaza, New York, NY 10004, U.S.A. Phone 1-800-SPRINGER, fax (201) 348-4505, e-mail orders-ny@springer-sbm. com, or visit www.springeronline.com. Apress Media, LLC is a California LLC and the sole member (owner) is Springer Science + Business Media Finance Inc (SSBM Finance Inc). SSBM Finance Inc is a **Delaware** corporation.

For information on translations, please e-mail editorial@apress.com; for reprint, paperback, or audio rights, please email bookpermissions@springernature.com.

Apress titles may be purchased in bulk for academic, corporate, or promotional use. eBook versions and licenses are also available for most titles. For more information, reference our Print and eBook Bulk Sales web page at http://www.apress.com/bulk-sales.

Any source code or other supplementary material referenced by the author in this book is available to readers on GitHub via the book's product page, located at www.apress.com/9781484261118. For more detailed information, please visit http://www.apress.com/source-code.

Printed on acid-free paper

Table of Contents

TABLE OF CONTENTS

TABLE OF CONTENTS

About the Author

John Kouraklis started exploring computers when he was 16 and since then has followed all the way from Turbo Pascal to the latest Delphi versions as a hobby initially and as a profession for most of his adult life. He has developed a wide range of applications, from financial software to reverse engineering tools, including an application for professional gamblers.

He is part of the Delphi community and participates in online communities, forums, and many other events. For example, he is active on Delphi-PRAXiS, which is perhaps the biggest English-speaking online forum about Delphi. John also has a personal website where he posts articles regularly. Lastly, he has written two more books about Delphi published by Apress.

About the Technical Reviewer

Dr. Holger Flick studied computer science at the Technical University of Dortmund and received his doctorate from the Faculty of Mechanical Engineering at the Ruhr-University Bochum. He has been programming with Delphi since 1996 and has always been active in the community. During and after his studies, he worked as a freelancer on numerous projects for Borland and was able to exchange ideas directly with many Delphi experts from Scotts Valley, CA. Mainly, he tested Delphi for the QA department, but also programmed database applications and web applications for the Borland Developer Network. Holger has also presented at conferences and seminars on various Delphi topics. His commitment and extensive knowledge of Delphi programming, gained through years of theoretical and practical work in the area of object-oriented programming with Delphi and other programming languages (e.g., C#, Objective-C), led to his appointment as the Embarcadero Delphi MVP in 2016. From 2013 to 2018, Dr. Holger Flick was responsible for the entire software and hardware architecture of a medium-sized business in Witten, Germany.

Among other things, he developed company-specific software solutions with Delphi. Since 2017, he presents products and solutions of TMS software as Chief Evangelist in the form of numerous technical articles, bilingual video tutorials, and leads through seminars. In 2019, he founded FlixEngineering LLC in the United States and is available for Delphi contracting of any kind. The next year, he self-published several books himself for web and desktop software development with Delphi.

Introduction

Delphi is a modern general-purpose programming language which enhances and supersedes Object Pascal. It is in the market for more than two decades now, and it is used in a wide range of applications. The language is maintained by Embarcadero and is backed by a large community of developers.

The language is versatile, it supports different programming paradigms, and it exhibits quick learning curve. It is easy to grasp the main and fundamental concepts and start coding straightaway. Naturally, as in every language, there is complexity down the line especially when advanced libraries are utilized.

This book offers a guide to the fundamentals. It takes people with no knowledge of the language all the way to what they need to know to start their journey in Delphi. By the end of this book, you will have enough knowledge to be able to read articles about Delphi and understand code of intermediate complexity. In short, this book offers a fast-track induction course to the language.

Who This Book Is For

The typical reader of this book is the newcomer to Delphi with basic knowledge of computer programming. The book offers all the necessary knowledge to get you started with Delphi and provides a wide range of references to allow you expand your knowledge.

After reading this book, you will be able to

- Discuss the fundamental elements of the language

- Appreciate the different programming paradigms that can be used in Delphi

- Write code to demonstrate the basic concepts of the language

Although the newcomer is in the center of this book, the experienced developer will benefit every time they are unsure or need a refresher on topics around the fundamentals of the language.

The Development Environment

The code in this book is written using the following environment:

- Embarcadero Delphi 10 Sydney (10.4)

- Microsoft Windows 10 Professional

I use the Professional edition, but there is nothing I do that exploits any features specific to this edition. The code can be tested using even the free Community Edition of Delphi. In fact, most of the code can be executed in other editions of Object Pascal.

There are some topics that utilize features found in specific versions of Delphi. Whenever this happens, I clearly flag the topics.

The Book's Structure

The book has five chapters. It starts with basic syntactical elements of the language and gradually introduces how core concepts of modern programming are managed in Delphi. Each chapter is independent to previous chapters, which means you can start reading the most suitable subject to your situation.

Chapter 1: Delphi Pascal

This chapter looks at Delphi as a programming language. It discusses the syntax and structure of the code, and it introduces the basic development workflow Delphi developers follow.

Chapter 2: Basics

The second chapter provides the fundamental knowledge a newcomer needs to get an understanding of how basic concepts in programming work in Delphi. Variables, data types, and generics are introduced.

Chapter 3: Looping, Conditional and Jump Statements

Managing the execution flow of code in Delphi is the topic of this chapter. Common structures like loops, conditional statements, and code jumps are covered to provide to the reader different ways to control logic in code.

Chapter 4: Procedures and Functions

In this chapter, we move to modular programming. We visit procedures and functions and investigate the way they are implemented and used in Delphi.

Chapter 5: Object-Oriented Programming (OOP)

OOP is one of the most fundamental and widespread paradigms in modern software development. In this chapter, we look at how OOP is done in Delphi and expand the discussion to cover interfaces, another core concept of contemporary programming.

Code Files

This book includes source code files that can be accessed via the
Download Source Code link located at www.apress.com/9781484261118.
The projects are named after the number of the chapter (ChapterXX) they
refer to. There is also a dedicated project group which loads all the projects
for all chapters. You can find it under the name DelphiQuickReference.
groupproj.

CHAPTER 1

Delphi Pascal

Delphi Pascal or, simply, Delphi is the most popular version of Object Pascal which, in turn, is an extension of the classic Pascal programming language (Cantu, 2016). This chapter introduces the basic concepts of the language.

Delphi As a Programming Language

Delphi is a general-purpose programming language. As a Pascal descendent, it draws its strong typing and syntactical characteristics from the original Pascal language developed by Niklaus Wirth in the early 1970s, but it, loosely, relates to the ISO standard Pascal (i.e., it is not a superset). Over the past decades, Delphi has evolved, and now it has features that makes it a modern programming language capable of building professional software in multiple platforms.

Syntax

If you look at Delphi source code, you will notice that it is dominated by words rather than symbols. Code appears inside a `begin...end` block rather than inside symbols like curly brackets (`{..}`) as in other languages.

Typically, code flows from top to bottom and from left to right. This implies that variables, objects, constants, and other elements need first to be declared before they are used (with the exception of forward declaration of classes).

© John Kouraklis 2020
J. Kouraklis, *Delphi Quick Syntax Reference*, https://doi.org/10.1007/978-1-4842-6112-5_1

Delphi is case insensitive, meaning that coding elements like variables, objects, methods, and the like can be declared in small or capital letters or in a combination of both. For example, the following declarations are all valid in Delphi: `delphiBook, delphi_Book, DelphiBook, DELPHIBOOK, delphiBOOK`. There are naming rules which prohibit the use of specific characters (e.g., an identifier cannot start with a number, etc.), but the limitations are very few, and, practically, when you code in Delphi, it is not common to come across them.

A notable difference with other languages is the operator to assign values to variables. In Delphi, a colon followed by the equal sign (`:=`) is used for this purpose, and the simple equal sign (`=`) is used to test equality in expressions.

Lastly, a convention that survived from the classic Pascal is the way the end of code line is declared in Delphi. Most of the lines of code end with a semicolon (`;`) with the exception of keywords (e.g., `begin...end`, `if...then`, `while...do`, etc.) and the last keyword in a code file. Every code file ends with the keyword end followed by a period (`end.`)

Programming Paradigms

Delphi is a fully developed object-oriented programming (OOP) language but does not force any specific development paradigm. You are free to use the OOP approach, but if, for some reasons, you prefer to use pure procedural programming, Delphi can fully support you. In fact, a huge part of the native libraries in Delphi come as procedures rather than embedded in objects and classes. This stands for Windows API calls, but, as the language is moving to cross-platform code, more libraries come in classes and records.

Compilation to Native Code

The final artifact of compilation of Delphi code is binary files with native code. In computing, this means that the final files represent machine code instead of an intermediate form like the one you find in virtual machine bytecode other languages produce. As a result, the executables run directly on top of the operating system without any translation layers between the executables and the underlying APIs of the operating systems.

Visual Applications

Delphi provides two out-of-the-box frameworks to support the development of visual applications: the Visual Component Library (VCL) and, starting from Delphi XE2, the FireMonkey (FMX) framework. VCL is used for Windows applications only, and FMX provides cross-platform components to build graphical user interfaces. Apart from VCL and FMX, there are third-party frameworks and libraries available to enrich the development of visual applications.

One Code Base for Multiple Platforms

One of the most distinguished characteristics of modern Delphi is the ability to produce binaries for multiple platforms from the same code base. At the time of writing, there are very few development tools in the market that truly support this. This means that, as a developer, you write code without any considerations as to which platform it will compile to, and Delphi takes the task to produce the appropriate executables or libraries for the platform of your choice. Currently, Delphi supports the following platforms: Windows 32-bit, Windows 64-bit, macOS 32-bit, macOS 64-bit, Android 32-bit, Android 64-bit, iOS, iOS 32-bit, iOS 64-bit, iOS Simulator, and Linux 64-bit. It is worth mentioning that although you can create applications for all the preceding platforms, the development is done on Windows only; that is, the compilers are Windows programs themselves.

Note   Although you can write cross-platform code without considering the details of the target platform, it is almost inevitable that your code, at some stage, will need to take advantage of the specificities of the target operating system. For that matter, Delphi allows you to fine-tune your code base using compiler directives and attributes.

Anatomy of a Delphi Program

A typical Delphi program can generate a number of different files depending on the nature of the program and the target platform.

Project Files

A *program* in Delphi has one source code file saved under the name of the application and with the .dpr extension. The code starts with the program keyword followed by the name of the application, and it has one main block of code enclosed in the begin..end keywords. The last end keyword is followed by a period (end.), and this signifies the end of the code file. Any text that appears after this generates a warning, but it is ignored by the compiler.

Delphi also generates a file with the .dproj extension. This file holds vital information about the cross-platform configurations, and it can also be used when the compilation of code is streamlined to MSBUILD.

There are a number of other support files with different extensions (e.g., .local, .deployproj) you may find, but they are not vital for the correct compilation of a Delphi program, or the compiler can regenerate them automatically.

Units

You can, very easily, create one big file and store all your code in it (with the exception of visual elements like forms and frames). Delphi will not complain and will compile your code correctly. However, this does not sound something that scales up easily when you write complex software. Instead, common practice suggests to organize your code in smaller separate files or modules as they are known in software engineering.

Delphi is a modular language and provides support to modules via *unit* files. In Pascal world, the term unit is used instead of module. The term module still exists in Delphi, and it refers to a special component (TDataModule) which sits in its own separate unit file. A unit is a separate code file, it has the .pas extension, and it is linked back to the project and is compiled to a binary file with the extension .dcu. DCUs are more important than the source code files because the compiler is able to use a .dcu file without the need to locate and access the corresponding .pas file. The downside is that DCU files are tightly linked to the version of the compiler that was used to create them. There were some exceptions in the past, but this is the general rule.

The following snippet shows the minimum elements you can find in a unit file (which, basically, does nothing). There are two distinct parts— interface and implementation. The interface section is the part of the unit that is visible to other units. For example, if you declare a variable in this section, it will be accessible to any other units that refer to this unit. On the other hand, any declarations made in the implementation section are only available in this unit and not outside it. When it comes to OOP, classes are typically declared in the interface section, and any method code should appear in the implementation section in the same unit. Of course, you can have the declaration and implementation of a class solely in the implementation section, but it will be accessible only within the unit.

```
unit QuickReference;

interface

// Declarations come here

implementation

// Declarations and Actual code come here

end.
```

This unit is named QuickReference, and the file name is and should be under the same name (QuickReference.pas). Delphi allows the use of dot notation in units which provides the ability to generate namespaces. As a result, you can save the unit under the name Quick.Reference.Delphi. pas. When you want to access the unit, you simply declare it using the keyword uses as follows:

```
uses
  Quick.Reference.Delphi;
```

The uses clause can appear either in the interface or the implementation part of a unit.

Forms and Frames

A *form* in Delphi is a representation of the typical window you see in visual applications. If you want to add a label or an edit field in the window, you add them in a form, and, when the code is executed, you see a window with the components.

Delphi creates two files for each form: a typical .pas file which contains all the declarations and any custom code you want to add to alter the behavior of the form and a .dfm (in VCL) or .fmx (in FireMonkey) file which holds information about the components in a form. A valid form needs both files.

Frames are very similar to forms with the difference that they do not represent stand-alone windows and they do not have system menus and icons. A frame can be embedded in forms or in other frames to build more complex and reusable user interfaces. In terms of files, frames use the same file structure as forms.

Delphi As Integrated Development Environment (IDE)

It is very possible to use a simple text editor to write Delphi code and then compile it using the compiler. This is the typical workflow of writing software in other programming languages.

However, the preceding approach is not scalable or even workable for the Delphi developer. Perhaps if you only write console applications, this may work, but the rule is that you write Delphi code in the integrated development environment that comes with the compiler provided by Embarcadero, the company behind Delphi. The IDE is branded as RAD Studio or Delphi IDE. This is a Windows application with a fully developed text editor (Figure 1-1), form designer (Figure 1-2), debugger, and project management features. The figures show the Delphi 10.4 IDE. The compiler and the form designer are very tightly coupled to the IDE, and, in practical terms, development in Delphi means writing code in RAD Studio.

Figure 1-1. *The Code View of Delphi IDE (Delphi 10.4 Sydney)*

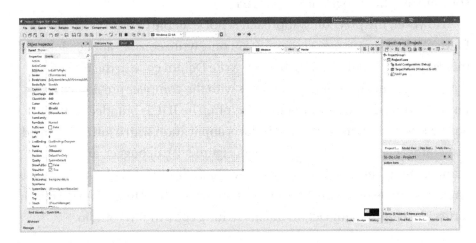

Figure 1-2. *The Form Designer in RAD Studio (Delphi 10.4 Sydney)*

The Delphi IDE is one of the most feature-rich development environments that exist in the market. If you would like to learn more, please read the official documentation for the latest release of the IDE (Embarcadero, n.d.) or download and install either the community edition or the trial version from the product's home page (Embarcadero, 2020).

A Simple Application (Console)

The simplest application you can create is a console application. This type of application does not have any graphical environment. It provides a text-only interface (Windows Console, macOS Terminal, etc.), and the interaction with the user is done via the keyboard and the display screen.

We are going to get started in Delphi by creating a console application.

1. Open Delphi IDE.

2. Select the *File ➤ New ➤ Console Application - Delphi* menu item.

   This will create a simple console application with the minimum code to support the development of a console application.

3. Save the project under the name Cheers.

4. We just want to print a simple message in the console. Go to the Code Editor by clicking on the tab at the bottom of the main part of the screen and add the following lines (in bold):

```
program Cheers;

{$APPTYPE CONSOLE}

{$R *.res}

uses
  System.SysUtils;

begin
  try
    { TODO -oUser -cConsole Main : Insert code here }
    Writeln('Hey Delphi, Cheers!');
    Writeln('Press Enter');
    Readln;
```

```
except
  on E: Exception do
    Writeln(E.ClassName, ': ', E.Message);
  end;
end.
```

5. Then either go to *Run* ➤ *Run* menu item, press *F9*
    or use the relevant button in the toolbar. This will
    compile and execute the code, and you will be able
    to see the output in a console window (Figure 1-3).
    Press Enter to close it and return to the IDE.

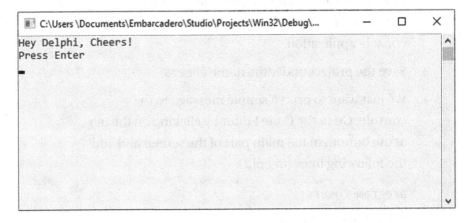

Figure 1-3. *Simple Output to Console*

Debugging is done inside the IDE as well. You can set a breakpoint at a
code line by clicking the gutter area in the text editor. When a breakpoint is
set, a red circle appears as shown in Figure 1-4. This area is the gutter area
of the editor.

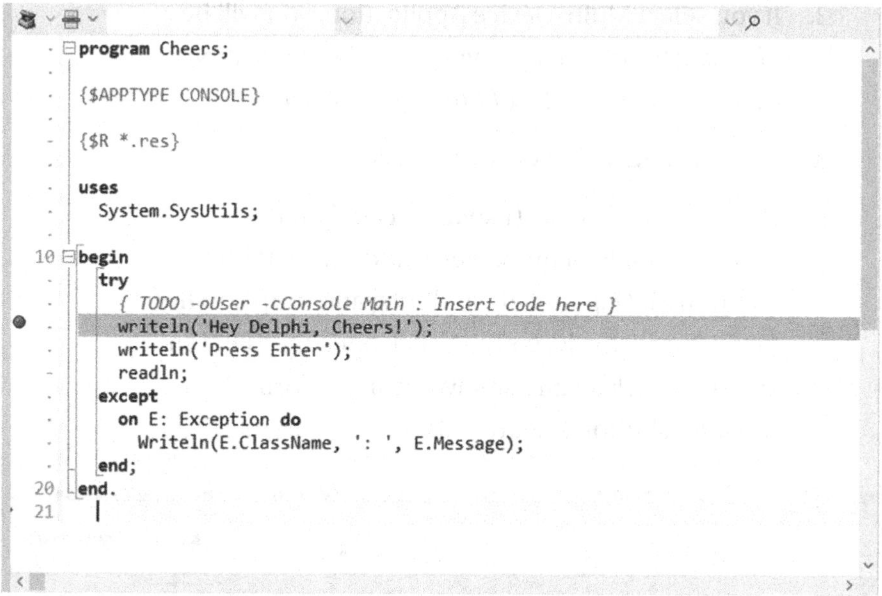

```
program Cheers;

{$APPTYPE CONSOLE}

{$R *.res}

uses
  System.SysUtils;

begin
  try
    { TODO -oUser -cConsole Main : Insert code here }
    writeln('Hey Delphi, Cheers!');
    writeln('Press Enter');
    readln;
  except
    on E: Exception do
      Writeln(E.ClassName, ': ', E.Message);
  end;
end.
```

Figure 1-4. *Breakpoints in the Delphi IDE*

Run again the project by pressing *F9*. This time the execution will stop at the line with the breakpoint, and you will be able to step through the code gradually by using the debugger buttons in the toolbar.

A Simple Application (Graphical)

In the previous section, we created a simple console application. This time we will create a graphical application to demonstrate how the IDE is used at a very basic level.

1. Select *File ➤ New ➤ Windows VCL Application – Delphi* or *Multi-Device Application – Delphi* from the main menu.

   The VCL, obviously, uses the VCL framework, and the Multi-Device Application uses FireMonkey (FMX).

11

2. If you select Multi-Device Application, you will be offered a list of different types of FMX applications (templates). Just select *Blank Application.*

3. Now the IDE will open the form designer.

4. Use the *Palette* panel (usually located on the right-hand side of the screen), find the TButton component (Figure 1-5), and drag and drop it to the form. Alternatively, you can click once the TButton and then click again somewhere in the form. This will add a button (Figure 1-6).

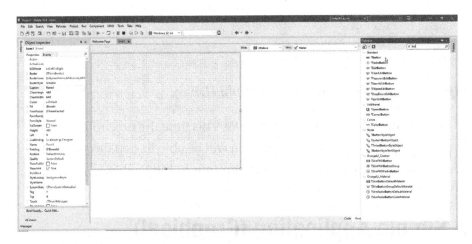

Figure 1-5. *Selecting TButton from the Palette*

5. Double-click the button. The designer will change to the code editor and will add some code. Then, add the following code:

```
procedure TForm1.Button1Click(Sender: TObject);
begin
    ShowMessage('Hey Delphi, Cheers!');
end;
```

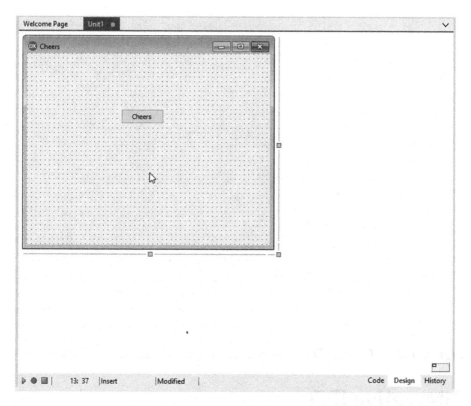

Figure 1-6. *Form Designer in Delphi IDE (Delphi 10.4 Sydney)*

6. Run the application and click the button. You are greeted with a message (Figure 1-7).

The preceding two simple applications demonstrate the most basic workflows in Delphi and present the basic editors (code, form) of the IDE.

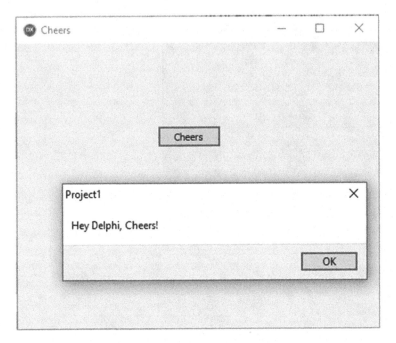

Figure 1-7. *VCL Application in Delphi IDE (Delphi 10.4 Sydney)*

Alternative IDEs

As mentioned earlier, Delphi development is done in Delphi IDE, which comes together with the compilers. The only other alternative to write pure Delphi code is to use Visual Studio Code with the OmniPascal extension (OmniPascal, 2020). OmniPascal adds to Visual Studio Code the capability to understand Delphi syntax and then to compile, debug, and run Delphi programs. The only downside is that it does not offer a form designer, which means that the Delphi IDE remains the only way to develop graphical applications in Delphi.

If we open the scope of the IDE and look at the domain of Object Pascal more broadly, there is another IDE worth mentioning. The Free Pascal community offers Lazarus (Lazarus, 2020) which is a cross-platform open source IDE. Lazarus is highly compatible with Delphi, but it is primarily made to support Free Pascal—another flavor of Object Pascal.

Delphi Style Guide

Delphi allows coders to use any naming conventions (with some exceptions as mentioned earlier) they feel work best for them and make their code readable especially when teams of developers are involved.

As it happens in every programming language, over the years, specific approaches to naming and other syntactical elements have emerged, and they are now commonly used among Delphi developers. For a complete guide, check this post (Calvert, n.d.). There are also some commonly found approaches to naming variables which are summarized in this piece (Riley, 2019).

Summary

In this chapter, we started with a very basic introduction of Delphi as a programming language. Then, we touched upon RAD Studio, the integrated environment that is, almost exclusively, used to develop Delphi software. In the next chapter, we review the basic elements of the language.

References

Calvert, C., n.d.. *Object Pascal Style Guide*. [Online] Available at: http://edn.embarcadero.com/article/10280#2.0 [Accessed 27 04 2020].

Cantu, M., 2016. *Object Pascal Handbook*. s.l.:s.n.

Embarcadero, 2020. *RAD Studio Product Page*. [Online] Available at: www.embarcadero.com/products/rad-studio [Accessed 08 04 2020].

Embarcadero, n.d. *RAD Studio Rio*. [Online] Available at: http://docwiki.embarcadero.com/RADStudio/Rio/en/Main_Page [Accessed 08 04 2020].

Lazarus, 2020. *Lazarus.* [Online] Available at: `www.lazarus-ide.org/` [Accessed 08 04 2020].

OmniPascal, 2020. *OmniPascal.* [Online] Available at: `www.omnipascal.com/` [Accessed 08 04 2020].

Riley, M., 2019. *What is the "A" prefix I see used on parameters?.* [Online] Available at: `https://capecodgunny.blogspot.com/2019/03/delphi-tip-of-day-what-is-a-prefix-i.html` [Accessed 27 04 2020].

CHAPTER 2

Basics

Variables

Variables, a term borrowed from mathematics, is what we use in software development to store data that change in the course of a program. It is, practically, hard to write code without using variables. Technically speaking, variables represent memory addresses, and they have two elements: an identifier and a data type.

The identifier is a convenient name that is used to access the value of the variable, and the data type defines what sort of data the variable holds. Delphi is a *strongly* and *statically* typed language. Strongly typed means that the developer defines the (data) type of the variable, and the variable cannot hold any other data type than the one defined; statically typed means that the data type is imposed at compile time rather than at runtime.

As an example, consider a variable that holds the age of a person. In Delphi, we define a variable using the keyword var followed by the identifier (name), a colon, and the data type. Traditionally, variables in Delphi are declared before the main block of a program or a method. Of course, all the conventions for naming identifiers and code lines apply (naming conventions, capitalization, and the use of semicolon at the end of the code line).

© John Kouraklis 2020
J. Kouraklis, *Delphi Quick Syntax Reference*, https://doi.org/10.1007/978-1-4842-6112-5_2

Building on the example from the previous chapter, we define our new variable as it is shown in the following code (for simplicity, I have removed the {..} text and the try...except block code):

```
program Cheers;

{$APPTYPE CONSOLE}

{$R *.res}

uses
  System.SysUtils;

var
  age: Integer;
begin
  Writeln('Hey Delphi, Cheers!');
  Writeln('Press Enter');
  Readln;
  age:=30;
end.
```

The age variable is defined outside the begin...end block by declaring the data type (Integer), and then it is used by assigning the value 30. Variables can be used as part of expressions like in every other programming language.

```
...
begin
  Writeln('Hey Delphi, Cheers!');
  Writeln('Press Enter');
  Readln;
```

```
age:=age + 10;
end.
```

Starting with Delphi 10.3 Rio, developers are able to declare variables inside block codes (inline variables) and assign values directly. The code now becomes as follows:

```
...
begin
  Writeln('Hey Delphi, Cheers!');
  Writeln('Press Enter');
  Readln;
  var age:Integer :=30;
end.
```

The age variable is valid in the specific block of code (begin...end). In most cases, the compiler is able to infer the type of the variable. Therefore, the code can be simplified even further, although if you are making your first steps in Delphi, you may find useful to explicitly declare the type of the variable as above. The declaration of an inline variable which allows the compiler to work out the type looks like this:

```
var age:=30;
```

A concept that comes together with variables (and constants) is the idea of variable scope. This means that variables are not valid and, thus, cannot be used anywhere in a code base. Instead, there are boundaries.

Typically, in Delphi, the scope is defined by the begin..end block closest to the declaration of the variable. In all the examples we have seen so far, we only have the main block of the console application. The variables are valid within this scope, but also the scope is global in these cases because there is only one block code.

As we add more knowledge around how the language works, we will see that the scope can be limited within a method (procedure/function), a loop statement, or a class. In some more advanced code, the scope can be the main block of a try...except/finally..end statement. Outside the scope, a variable is not recognizable by the compiler.

Data Types

Integer

In Delphi, there is a good number of integer types that can be used depending on how big you expect the number to be, whether you want to carry the sign or not (signed/unsigned) and the target platform of the application (Tables 2-1 and 2-2).

Table 2-1. *Platform-Independent Integer Types*

Platform-Independent Integer	Type
ShortInt (Int8)	Signed 8-bit
SmallInt (Int16)	Signed 16-bit
Integer (FixedInt)	Signed 32-bit
Int64	Signed 64-bit
Byte	Unsigned 8-bit
Word	Unsigned 16-bit
Cardinal (FixedUInt)	Unsigned 32-bit
UInt64	Unsigned 64-bit

Table 2-2. *Platform-Dependent Integer Types*

Platform-Dependent Integer	Platform	Type
NativeInt (Integer)	32-bit (All Platforms)	Signed 32-bit
NativeInt (Int64)	64-bit (All Platforms)	Signed 64-bit
NativeUInt (Cardinal)	32-bit (All Platforms)	Unsigned 32-bit
NativeUInt (UInt64)	64-bit (All Platforms)	Unsigned 64-bit
LongInt (Integer)	32-bit (All Platforms) 64-bit (Windows)	Signed 32-bit
LongInt (Int64)	64-bit (iOS, Linux)	Signed 64-bit
LongWord (Cardinal)	32-bit (All Platforms) 64-bit (Windows)	Unsigned 32-bit
LongWord (UInt64)	64-bit (All Platforms)	Unsigned 64-bit

Char

The Char data type represents a single character. For historical reasons, when Unicode characters and strings were added to Delphi, a whole range of char (and string) types was introduced to accommodate the different requirements of non-Unicode and Unicode characters (and strings). This led to some confusion among developers.

Modern Delphi development does not really look at such differences (unless a very old compiler is used), and the data type char can be safely used in desktop and mobile applications to handle Unicode characters.

Boolean

Boolean values represent two states: True and False. As in the case of char type, there are more than one Boolean types to facilitate communication with other languages and operating systems, but, again, the vast majority of code does not use them. True Boolean value translates to 1 and false to 0.

Enumerated Types

Enumerated types need to be defined before used as data types in variables. They are truly custom data type to fit the needs of the developer. The values bear no meaning to the compiler and can be used to improve readability and increase abstraction. Enumerated type can be defined as in the following examples:

```
type
  TAnswer = (aYes, aNo);
  TChapter = (cChapter01, cChapter02, cChapter3, cChapter4);
```

The definition should appear outside the main block..end or an application or a method. Once they are defined, a variable of TChapter type is very easily declared:

```
var
  consent: TAnswer;
  currentChapter: TChapter;
```

and then we use them as before:

```
begin
  consent:=aYes;
  currentChapter:=cChapter02;
end.
```

Subrange

Subrange is a very handy data type. It provides the ability to declare data types as a range (`Low..High`), and it is related to another (predefined) data type. The code snippet that follows defines a subrange that represents the adult ages and some chapters from the `TChapter` enumerated type:

```
Type
  TMyCoinsAge = 10..High(Byte);
  TMainPart = cChapter02..cChapter04;
```

Subranges can also resolve expressions:

```
type
  TExperimentTemp = -10..3 * (20 + 5);
```

Real

This data type represents a floating-point number (decimal) of different precision. Table 2-3 presents the available real data types in Delphi.

Table 2-3. Floating-Point Data Types

Type	Platform	Significant Decimal Digits	Size (Bytes)	Notes
Real48	All platforms	11–12	6	Legacy data type
Single	All platforms	7–8	4	
Real (Double)	All platforms	15–16	8	
Extended	32-bit Intel (Windows)	10–20	10	
Extended	32-bit Intel (all platforms)	10–20	16	
Extended	64-bit Intel (Linux)	10–20	16	
Extended	All other CPUs and platforms	15–16	8	
Comp	All platforms	10–20	8	Legacy data type
Currency	All platforms	10–20	8	64-bit integer with 4 decimal points. Used in monetary calculations

Strings

Strings represent a sequence of characters. The transition to Unicode led to a number of string data types. Similarly to the case of char, modern development does not consider the different types, and we just use the type string (unless an older compiler is used or there are other more specific requirements).

```
...
var
  name: string;
begin
  name:='Delphi';
  var surname:='Quick Reference Guide';
end.
```

As you can see from the preceding code, strings in Delphi are enclosed in single quotes (' ').

If you want to print a single quote, then you have to *escape* it by using two single quotes (not double quote mark) as in the following example:

```
begin
  ...
  Writeln('Delphi''s fantastic world!');
  ...
end.
```

Delphi carries the same philosophy as the original Pascal language in regard to the index of the first letter of a string; string starts from 1 rather than 0; but this is only for Windows. When more platforms were added, the decision was made to revert to the most common indexing style in the world of software and assign the value 0 to the first character of a string (except for macOS which uses the Windows convention). Therefore, if you want to access the first character of name, on Windows you write this:

```
Writeln(name[1]);
```

but on any other platform, you access it this way:

```
Writeln(name[0]);
```

This approach means that you need to differentiate the code based on the platform you are compiling. There is another way to go around this. You can use the function Low to allow the compiler to figure out the correct starting index:

```
Writeln(name[low(name)]);
```

The manipulation of strings (e.g., concatenating, extracting substrings, finding the position of a substring, etc.) is supported in all platforms by simple calls to methods. For example, if you want to find the position of a substring in a given string, the following call will do the job and return 14 on Windows and 13 on all other platforms:

```
Writeln(Pos('Reference', 'Delphi Quick Reference'));
```

Although this code works, in the cross-platform world, the use of standard methods to manipulate strings is not recommended. Instead, Delphi comes with a new set of methods optimized for speed and platform compatibility and goes under TStringHelper in System.SysUtils unit. These methods are accessed using the dot notation (.) on a string. Therefore, the preceding code now becomes

```
Writeln('Delphi Quick Reference'.IndexOf('Reference'));
```

Due to the fluent approach (dot notation), several methods can be chained to manipulate strings. For example, check this code snippet:

```
Writeln('Delphi Quick Reference'
                        .Substring(0,'Delphi'.Length)
                        .ToUpper);
```

This code first applies the SubString methods on 'Delphi Quick Reference' string starting from index 0. It extracts as many characters as the length of string 'Delphi' using the Length method. Then, it converts the extracted part to uppercase using ToUpper method and prints out the word DELPHI.

As mentioned, TStringHelper is the modern approach to string manipulation, and it should replace the use of older methods as they may be deprecated in future versions (Embarcadero, 2015).

Sets

Sets are an extremely convenient way to manage groups of elements of the same data type. A set is defined in relation to an enumerated data type. Earlier when we discussed enumerated types, we defined TChapter. Now, we need a set to represent the chapters we have read. We do this with the following declarations:

```
type
  TChapter = (cChapter01, cChapter02, cChapter3, cChapter4);
  TChaptersRead = set of TChapter;

var
  progress: TChaptersRead;

begin
  progress:=[cChapter01, cChapter02];
end.
```

This time we declare TChaptersRead to represent a set of chapters, and we assign the progress variable to this particular type. Then, populating progress with chapters is a very simple step.

In fact, the power of sets becomes apparent when we consider the easiness of manipulating that comes with the use of addition and subtraction operators.

Consider the case of user permissions. We want to create a group of users and assign permissions like create a user, read the details of a user, update user's details, and delete a user. We declare the enumerated types:

```
type
  TPermission = (pCreate, pRead, pUpdate, pDelete);
  TGroup = set of TPermission;
```

Next, we define a new variable to hold TGroup data:

```
var
  admin: TGroup;
```

Now we clean the group (although it is not necessary):

```
admin:=[];
```

Then, we are ready to add permissions to the admin group:

```
begin
  admin:=[];
  admin:=admin + [pCreate];
  admin:=admin + [pUpdate..pDelete];
end.
```

As the code illustrates, the addition of new permissions is very simple, and the code is highly readable.

If we need to check whether a permission exists in admin group, we can use the in operator:

```
writeln(pCreate in admin);
```

Arrays

Arrays in programming languages are sequences of elements of the same type. The order of the elements is defined by an index, and the first element is at index 0 (zero-based arrays). In Delphi, arrays can be declared in two ways depending on whether the size of the array is known or not.

When you know the size of the array, you can declare it as follows:

```
var
  arrStatic: array[0..9] of string;
```

This type of array is called *static array,* and you can straightaway access the elements of the array by referring to their indices:

```
begin
  arrStatic[0]:='Delphi';
  arrStatic[4]:='Quick Reference';
end.
```

Note that the elements in the array contain arbitrary values; do not assume that they are *empty* (whatever this means for the type of data the array holds).

Static arrays need not be of one dimension; Delphi supports multidimensional arrays by concatenating arrays as in the following snippets:

```
var
  arrDual: array[0..9] of array[0..9] of string;
  arrDualAlt: array[0..9, 0..9] of string;
  arrMulti: array[0..9, 0..9, 0..9] of string;
```

Both 2x2 declarations work and are equivalent. As you can see in the code, you can have truly multidimensional arrays, and the elements can be accessed by attaching the dimension indices one next to the other. For example, if we want to access the third element, in the second row at the seventh position of arrMulti, we write

```
arrMulti[3][2][7]:='Multidimensional Array';
```

or simply

```
  arrMulti[3, 2, 7]:='Multidimensional Array';
```

If you are not able to determine the size of the area beforehand, you can define a *dynamic array* of a specific type by omitting the indices:

```
var
  arrDynamic: array of string;
```

Because arrDynamic is a dynamic array, we need to specify the size of the array before we access any elements. We do this with SetLength:

```
SetLength(arrDynamic, 10);
arrDynamic[0]:='Delphi';
```

If you don't use SetLength, any attempts to access the elements of the array will generate an error because memory slots are not yet being allocated.

Similar to multidimensional static arrays, multidimensional dynamic arrays can be declared.

```
var
  arrDynamicMulti: array of array of String;
```

Again, the length needs to be defined before you attempt to access the elements.

```
begin
  SetLength(arrDynamicMulti, 10, 10);
  arrDynamicMulti[5][3]:='Quick Reference';
  Writeln(arrDynamicMulti[5][3]);
end.
```

A very interesting implication of static and dynamic arrays is that you can combine them and declare an array with one or more known dimensions and other unknown ones. For example, the following first statement defines a ten-element array which has expandable number of strings per element. Similarly, the second statement declares an array of unknown number of elements of ten strings:

```
var
  arrMixed: array[0..9] of array of string;
  arrMixedReverse: array of array[0..9] of string;
```

You access the elements by setting the correct length first as we did before:

```
SetLength(arrMixed[0], 10);
arrMixed[0][5]:='Delphi';

SetLength(arrMixedReverse, 10);
arrMixedReverse[3][5]:='Quick Reference';
```

An alternative way to declare an array is to create a new data type:

```
type
  TMixedArray = array[0..9] of array of string;
```

Then, you define a new variable of this type and use it as normal:

```
var
  arrMixedAlt: TMixedArray;
begin
  SetLength(arrMixedAlt[3], 10);
  arrMixedAlt[3, 3]:='Delphi';
end.
```

Records

Records (or structures as they are called in other languages) provide the ability to group elements (fields) of different types together. We define a record in the types section, and then we declare a variable.

```
type
  TBook = record
    Title: string;
    Pages: Integer;
  end;
```

```
var
  thisBook: TBook;

begin
  thisBook.Title:='Delphi Quick Reference Book';
  thisBook.Pages:=100;
end.
```

Records are very useful when you have data structures with common fields and additional fields that depend on conditions. In the TBook example, we can have different formats of a book: a hard copy and a PDF version. In the first case, we care to know whether the book is in stock, and in the second case, we need to provide a download URL. In this scenario, it is obvious that the two cases are mutually exclusive; when you have a hard copy, you do not need the download URL.

We declare a new data type to differentiate the different book formats, and then we use the case statement within the record declaration. Note that if a field of string type is declared in the case options, you need to provide the length of the string.

```
type
  TBookFormat = (bfHardCopy, bfPDF);
  TBook = record
    Title: string;
    Pages: Integer;
    case Format: TBookFormat of
      bfHardCopy: (InStock: Boolean);
      bfPDF: (DownloadURL: string[100]);
  end;
```

Then, we use Format to activate the different fields.

```
begin
  thisBook.Title:='Delphi Quick Reference Book';
  thisBook.Pages:=100;
```

```
  thisBook.Format:=bfHardCopy;
  thisBook.InStock:=true;

  thisBook.Format:=bfPDF;
  thisBook.DownloadURL:='http://';
end.
```

Records share some common functionality with classes—but they are not the same. Records have a default constructor that is called automatically whenever the record is used. However, records do not implement destructors.

To demonstrate the use of constructors, let's declare a record that generates a password. We want to be able to pass a salt value (which in fact will not do anything meaningful in this example but will get the point across). Note that when you define new record constructors, they must carry a parameter; in other words, you cannot have a parameter-less constructor in records, and you cannot override the default one.

```
type
  TRandomPassword = record
    Password: string;
  public
    constructor Create (const aSalt: string);
  end;

constructor TRandomPassword.Create(const aSalt: string);
begin
  inherited;
  Password:=aSalt + '$%HJKFbmnmn';
end;

var
  password: TRandomPassword;
```

```
begin
  password:=TRandomPassword.Create('123');
  writeln(password.Password);
end.
```

Earlier I mentioned that you cannot override the default parameter-less constructor and that records do not have destructors. Delphi 10.4 introduced a feature called *custom managed records*. Although you are not able to override the default constructor and destructor, you can add initialization and finalization code via the relevant operators. The following code shows how custom managed records work. First, we declare the Initialization and Finalization operators.

```
type
  TRandomPasswordCustom = record
    Password: string;
  public
    class operator Initialize (out Dest: TRandomPasswordCustom);
    class operator Finalize (var Dest: TRandomPasswordCustom);
  end;

class operator TRandomPasswordCustom.Initialize (out Dest:
TRandomPasswordCustom);
begin
  Dest.Password:='$%HJKFbmnmn';
end;

class operator TRandomPasswordCustom.Finalize (var Dest:
TRandomPasswordCustom);
begin
  Writeln('Record is finalised')
end;
```

Initialization and Finalization are special types of methods (operators). Note that they both need a reference to the record itself via the Dest parameter.

We use TRandomPasswordCustom the usual way as with the classic records.

```
var
  customPassword: TRandomPasswordCustom;
begin
  ...
  // *** This works in Delphi 10.4 and above ***
  Writeln('Custom Record Password: ' +
                        customPassword.Password);
end.
```

If you run the code, Password is automatically initialized to the desired value. We do not need any extra steps when we use the record in our code.

Pointers

The declaration of variables, the association to specific data types, and the ability to access the value of the variable at specific memory address are all left to the compiler. It is pretty much what is happening under the hood when variables are used—and they are used a lot. In the vast majority of programming—even in complex programming—this is more than enough; it is efficient and productive.

However, there are cases that can be achieved by directly accessing the memory where the value of a variable is stored instead of allowing the compiler to manage this. Such cases are achieved by declaring a pointer variable (pointers).

In the part with the records, we declared password, a variable to hold an instance of TRandomPassword. Let's find out the address of the variable.

```
var
  password: TRandomPassword;
  passAddress: Pointer;
begin
  password:=TRandomPassword.Create('123');
  ...
  passAddress:=@password;
  writeln(integer(passAddress).ToHexString);
end.
```

We first declare passAddress, a pointer variable, and point it to the address of password. This is achieved by using the @ (address) operator. Instead of @, you can use the method Addr. When you run the code, you will see the address in hex format (004FA7E0 in my system).

There is much more into pointers as the topic is very complicated and yet very powerful. This is an introductory book, and, therefore, diving into pointers is out of its scope. There are many good resources available online with this blog post (Velthuis, 2019) by late Rudy Velthuis, a legendary figure in Delphi world, being one of the best explanations available.

Variant

In the beginning of this chapter, we saw that Delphi is a strongly typed language, meaning that a variable is declared to represent a specific data type. The Variant data type circumvents this requirement and allows developers to assign different types of data that are being automatically converted at runtime.

Consider the following:

```
var
  flex: Variant;
begin
  flex:= 30;
```

```
Writeln('Flex as integer: ', flex);
flex:= 'Thirty';
Writeln('Flex as string: ', flex);
end.
```

We declare flex as Variant, and in the beginning, we assign an integer. Then, we are able to assign a value of a totally different type. Variants, although flexible structures, are slow, and they should not be used widely or as a replacement to proper variable declarations. They are used for specific purposes (e.g., COM programming on Windows) and, as with pointers, require some level of expertise and experience to utilize them safely.

Generics

Generic programming allows the declaration and manipulation of variables by not specifying the exact type until needed. The biggest advantage of such approach is that algorithms can be created in an abstract (generic) way that works with a number of data types. This is an attempt to reduce duplication. This concept is found under the same term in other languages. Additionally, the terms *template* and *parameterized types* are also common.

We define generics using a set of angle brackets (<T>), where T is used to define the exact data type of interest. The letter T is more a convention than a requirement. As an example, let's look at the declaration of the dynamic arrays we used earlier and how we can take advantage of generics.

We declared arrStatic as in the following lines:

```
var
  arrDynamic: array[0..9] of string;
```

In a more generic way, we would write:

```
var
  genArray: TArray<string>;
```

We declare genArray to be of TArray<string> type. Then, we would treat genArray as we would treat a classic dynamic array. Delphi comes with a number of predefined types of arrays for different data types (e.g., TStringDynArray, TBooleanDynArray, etc.), and we can declare multidimensional arrays by declaring the generic type T to be of another array. In the following example, arrTypedDual demonstrates how this can be done:

```
var
  arrTyped: TArray<string>; // or, arrTyped: TStringDynArray
  arrTypedDual: TArray<TArray<string>>;
begin
  SetLength(arrTyped, 10);
  arrTyped[3]:='Typed';

  SetLength(arrTypedDual, 10, 10);
  arrTypedDual[5, 5]:='Typed Dual';
end.
```

The real advantage of generics comes when we combine them with records (and classes). We are going to implement a record that receives a generic data type and logs (prints out) the type of the generic.

Let's declare the record which has only one method.

```
type
  TLogType<T> = record
    procedure logType;
  end;
```

```
procedure TLogType<T>.logType;
begin
   ...
end;
```

I have omitted the actual implementation for two reasons: firstly, we have not talked yet about methods in Delphi and, secondly, printing out the type of T requires some deeper knowledge of Run-Time Type Information (RTTI). It is not as complicated as it sounds as this is done, literally, in one line. At this stage, it would only destruct us from focusing on generics. In the code that comes with the book, you can find the full implementation.

Having declared TLogType<T>, we define variables that pass different data types to TLogType.

```
var
   logInteger: TLogType<integer>;
   logString: TLogType<string>;
   logRandomPassword: TLogType<TRandomPassword>;

begin
   logInteger.logType;
   logString.logType;
   logRandomPassword.logType;
end.
```

The preceding code will print the types of logInteger, logString, and logRandomPassword (Integer, String, TRandomPassword). As you can observe, it has significantly increased the reusability of our code.

Generics is a very flexible feature, and there is way more that you can do with them. For a more detailed discussion, visit the relevant wiki page in this source (Embarcadero, 2015) and read Nick Hodges's book (Hodges, 2014).

Constants

Constants are values that coders define, and they remain unchanged during the execution of an application. In Delphi, constants are defined using the const keyword and the equal sign:

```
const
  PUBLISHER = 'Apress';
```

You can include expressions in constants that can be resolved by the compiler; that is, they can be evaluated without the execution of the program. Examples of constants with expressions can be seen in the following snippet:

```
const
  EXTENDED_SHIFT = 12;
  WAGE_PER_HOUR = 10;
  NORMAL_DAILY_WAGE = NORMAL_SHIFT * WAGE_PER_HOUR;
  EXTENDED_DAILY_WAGE = EXTENDED_SHIFT * WAGE_PER_HOUR *
                                                    1.30;
```

More complex constants that include arrays and records can be defined, but the data types need to be explicitly declared.

```
const
  CHAPTER_TITLES : array[0..2] of string =
                ('Introduction','Chapter 1','Chapter 2');
```

On a more technical note, when a constant is declared, Delphi reserves the required memory slot, and then it treats it as a variable. This means that you can change the value of a constant in the code. This may defeat the concept of a constant, but it is not uncommon in programming languages. In the C-family languages, this treatment is called static variable.

Comments

There are four ways to add comments to the code:

- Using //: This type of comment is interpreted as a line comment; that is, anything after this is discarded by the compiler.

- Using (*..*): This is a multiline comment identifier.

- Using {..}: This is also a multiline comment identifier.

- Using ///: This is a special type of comments (documentation comments) and is used to document the code in such way that the IDE and documentation software understand. In order to work, it follows specific structure and pattern.

Comments are ignored by the compiler and can appear anywhere in a Delphi unit. The use of (*..*) and {..} allows for multiline and nested comments as in the following example:

```
// Line comment
{ Some other comment}
(* Yet another comment type *)

(* Comments in
            Multiple lines
      { and in multiple levels }
*)
```

Summary

In this chapter, we looked at the most fundamental elements that define Delphi—variables, data types, constants, and comments—and discussed some ways to use them. The next chapter focuses on ways to control the order of execution.

References

Embarcadero, 2015. *Overview of Generics*. [Online] Available at: `http://docwiki.embarcadero.com/RADStudio/Sydney/en/Overview_of_Generics` [Accessed 03 06 2020].

Embarcadero, 2015. *System.SysUtils.TStringHelper*. [Online] Available at: `http://docwiki.embarcadero.com/Libraries/Sydney/en/System.SysUtils.TStringHelper` [Accessed 03 06 2020].

Hodges, N., 2014. *Coding in Delphi*. s.l.:Nepeta Enterprises.

Velthuis, R., 2019. *Addressing Pointers*. [Online] Available at: `http://rvelthuis.de/articles/articles-pointers.html` [Accessed 27 04 2020].

CHAPTER 3

Looping, Conditional and Jump Statements

Loops

Loops allow a chunk of code to be executed as long as a control condition is valid (true) or for specific number of iterations. In Delphi, you manage loops either by using a while, a repeat, or a for statement.

While Statement

A while..do statement executes the designated code as long as the condition that appears between the keywords while and do (control condition) is true. The evaluation of the control statement is done in the very beginning of the loop, which means that the relevant code may or may not be executed at all.

```
var
  whileControl: Integer;
begin
  whileControl:=0;
  while whileControl <=10 do
```

© John Kouraklis 2020
J. Kouraklis, *Delphi Quick Syntax Reference*, https://doi.org/10.1007/978-1-4842-6112-5_3

```
  begin
    writeln(whileControl);
    whileControl:=whileControl + 1;
  end;
end.
```

In the preceding code, the while loop first evaluates the expression whileControl<=10, and if true it goes ahead and executes the statements in the begin..end block. If you change the initial value of whileControl to anything bigger than 10, the code in the begin..end will not be executed.

There are two points to emphasize. Firstly, in while loops, we can change the control variable (whileControl) because the control condition is evaluated at the beginning of every iteration. Secondly, in while loops, the code that is executed is the statement that appears immediately after the do keyword. In the following code, only the writeln(whileControl) will be executed:

```
begin
  whileControl:=0;
  while whileControl <=10 do
    writeln(whileControl);
  whileControl:=whileControl + 1;
end.
```

Consequently, the control variable will never be incremented and the while loop will never stop. To deal with this, we use a begin..end block as in the first example. In general, the use of such blocks is good programming practice; it costs nothing in terms of compiling load, and it makes the code far more readable.

Repeat Statement

A repeat..until statement executes the designated statements that appear between the keywords repeat and until as long as the control statement is *not* true. In other words, the iterations stop when the control statement is true. The control statement follows the until keyword. The direct implication of this construct is that the code is executed *at least* once before the control condition is evaluated.

As an example, let's use the same condition we used in the case of the while statement:

```
begin
  whileControl:=0;
  repeat
    writeln(whileControl);
    whileControl:=whileControl + 1;
  until whileControl<=10;
end.
```

In the beginning, the control variable is 0. The code enters the repeat block and executes the two lines of code until it hits the until keyword. Then, it evaluates the whileControl<=10 statement. In this very first iteration, the statement is true and, therefore, the iterations finish. As a result, the code is executed only once.

If we change the control condition to whileControl>=10, the code will run a number of times. As mentioned earlier, the evaluation is done at the end of the first pass. This makes the loop to be executed 10 times rather than 11 as in the case of while. This is a consequence of the way the control statements are evaluated. Another difference with the while statement is that all the statements that appear in the repeat..until block will be executed.

For Statement

The For statement executes statements the exact number of iterations you specify. You do this by providing an initial and a final value to a counter variable instead of explicitly declaring the number of iterations. For example, if you want a block of code to run 10 times, you pass to for the initial value of 1 and the final value of 10. The code will run

$$finalValue - initialValue + 1 \text{ times}$$

$$\text{or, } 10 - 1 + 1 = 10 \text{ times}$$

If the final value is smaller than the initial value, then the for loop is not executed at all. The next code chunk shows how for is used:

```
var
  forControl: integer;
begin
  for forControl := 1 to 10 do
    writeln(forControl);
end.
```

Note that we need to declare the control variable the usual way we follow for every other variable; that is, by declaring it outside the main begin..end block. The data type of this variable must be the same as or assignment compatible to the structure you iterate. For example, if you iterate through integers, the control variable must be declared as integer. Delphi 10.3 introduced inline variables, and this opened the possibility to use them in a for loop as follows:

```
for var newForControl := 1 to 10 do
  writeln(newForControl);
```

In order to make a for loop execute in the case you have smaller final value than the initial one, then use the keyword downto instead of to.

```
for forControl := 10 downto 1 do
  Writeln(forControl);
```

The number of iterations is evaluated at the beginning of the loop and only once, and you are not allowed to change the value of the control variable (forControl) within the for loop.

When you iterate more complex structures like arrays or collections, you can use the very convenient in syntax as you can observe in the following lines:

```
var
  forArray: array[0..9] of Integer =
                        (10,20,30,40,50,60,70,80,90,100);
  forINControl: integer;
begin
  for forINControl in forArray do
    writeln(forINControl);
end.
```

We declare an array which can be either static or dynamic. For simplicity, I declared and initialized a static array in this example. Then, we need the variable forINControl to use in the for loop. The variable must be of the same data type as the elements of the array or the collection (integer). Finally, the for..in form is used to iterate through the elements of the array.

In Delphi 10.3 and above, the inline variable declaration can also be used as shown in the following example. With this approach, you do not have to declare the type of the control variable because the compiler is able to infer it automatically.

```
for var newForINControl in forArray do
  writeln(newForINControl);
```

Conditional Statements

Conditional statements allow the execution of code when a statement (or condition) is true, following the usual pattern we saw in `while` and `repeat` statements. In Delphi, conditional statements take the form of `if` or `case` statements.

If Statement

In its simplest form, `If` statements follow the natural language: *if* something is valid, *then* this happens.

```
var
  grade: integer;
begin
  grade:=10;
  if grade > 5 then
    Writeln('Greater than 5');
end.
```

In this case, the expression `grade > 5` is true, and the next line is executed. `If` executes only the next line of code; thus, if more lines need to run when the expression is valid, you need to use a `begin..end` block as in the following example:

```
if grade > 5 then
begin
  writeln('Greater than 5');
  writeln('You pass');
end;
```

Following the natural language analogy, the statement can be expanded to include the alternative course of action: *if* something is valid, *then* this happens; *otherwise* something else happens. This *otherwise* branch is implemented in Delphi with the else keyword.

```
if grade > 5 then
begin
  writeln('Greater than 5');
  writeln('You pass');
end
else
  writeln('You fail');
```

Note that the statement right before else should not end with a semicolon (;). You can freely nest if-then-else statements to cover cases relevant to your code as in the following snippet:

```
if grade > 5 then
begin
  writeln('Greater than 5');
  writeln('You pass');
end
else
begin
  if grade = 5 then
    writeln('This is borderline pass')
  else
    if grade >=3 then
      writeln('This can be improved easily')
    else
      writeln('This is of very poor quality');
end;
```

Case Statement

A case statement is an alternative approach to if statements and provides a more readable form of selecting routes of action based on an expression. However, if is much more flexible in terms of what sort of expressions you can have. Case selects a path if the expression is of ordinal type, that is, the possible options can be somehow presented in an order. The previous if-then-else statements with the grade can, now, be expressed as follows:

```
begin
  case grade of
    0..2: writeln('This is of very poor quality');
    3..4: writeln('This can be improved easily');
       5: writeln('This is borderline pass');
  else
    begin
      writeln('Greater than 5');
      writeln('You pass');
    end;
  end;
end.
```

We have put the grades in order and took appropriate action for each level of grade. As it is demonstrated, you can have a single ordinal value (e.g., 5) or a range of values (e.g., 0..2). Case supports an optional else branch to allow you to cover a range of options in a collective way. Note that each option should include one and only statement or a block of statements wrapped with begin..end.

Practically, the only data types you cannot use in a case expression are strings and very long integers (64-bit). For the strings, there is a very useful method named IndexStr in System.StrUtils unit. It receives a string and an array of strings as parameters and returns the index of the array element that matches the string.

```
case IndexStr('Pass', ['Fail', 'Pass', 'Honors']) of
  0: writeln('You fail');
  1: writeln('You pass');
  2: writeln('You pass with honors');
end;
```

IndexStr will look for the value Pass in the array of the string (Fail, Pass, Honors) and return the relevant index, which is 1 in this case. Then, the case statement will execute the code linked to this index. This is an example that shows how to convert arbitrary values to ordinal values.

Jump Statements

Jump statements are commands that allow you to change the flow of the execution of your code. They usually appear in loop statements (while, repeat, for). In Delphi, there are four such statements: exit, break, continue, goto.

Exit Statement

When an exit statement is triggered, the code leaves the current execution block. If it is in the main execution block, the application ends. In procedures and functions, exit statement will cause the execution of the code to return to the point where the procedure or the function was called, as we will see in the next chapter.

```
begin
  if grade = 5 then
    Exit;
end.
```

Break Statement

A Break statement inside a loop causes the loop to stop and the code to resume at the point right after the last statement of the loop.

```
var
  loopVar: integer;
begin
  loopVar:=0;
  while loopVar<=10 do
  begin
    if loopVar = 3 then
      Break;
    loopVar:=loopVar + 1;
  end;
  writeln(loopVar);
end.
```

In the preceding code, the while loop is set to run until loopVar reaches the value of 10, but the break statement will interrupt it when the variable goes to 3.

Continue Statement

Continue is similar to Break in the sense that it breaks a loop and does not allow more lines to be executed. The difference is that it does not cause the execution of the code to leave the loop, but instead it moves the execution to the next iteration. The following code will skip value 3 because when loopVar is equal to 3, continue takes the execution back to the while statement to allow the next iteration.

```
var
  loopVar: integer;
begin
  while loopVar<=10 do
  begin
    loopVar:=loopVar + 1;
    if loopVar = 3 then
      Continue;
    writeln(loopVar);
  end;
end.
```

Goto Statement

Goto statement is another way to alter the normal execution flow of the code and direct it elsewhere. In order to use goto, you need to define a label using the label keyword outside the begin..end block.

```
var
  loopVar: integer;
label
  outsideWhile;
begin
  loopVar:=0;
  while loopVar<=10 do
  begin
    loopVar:=loopVar + 1;
    if loopVar = 3 then
      goto outsideWhile;
    writeln(loopVar);
  end;
```

```
outsideWhile:
  writeln('Now outside while with a goto statement');
end.
```

When `loopVar` reaches the value of 3, `goto` will redirect the execution to `outsideWhile` label, and thus the last `writeln` statement will be executed.

The use of labels to redirect the execution of code is not considered a modern programming approach; in fact, the use of `goto` today indicates bad programming practices and code of low quality. Delphi supports it due to legacy ties to traditional Pascal.

Summary

This chapter offered a review of the most commonly used statements to support and control the execution of code. It visited loops and conditional and jump statements—all very important elements to develop more structured and meaningful code. In the next chapter, we look at how procedural programming is implemented in Delphi and ways to write more complex code.

CHAPTER 4

Procedures and Functions

Modular programming in Delphi is implemented by handling two types of routines (or methods): procedures and functions. The two types have many similarities and one difference; functions return a value to the point of call. The idea is that the code uses this value to proceed with the algorithm it implements. Procedures just execute the code. This is the rule; however, as we will see, there is a way to use procedures to modify values at the point of call.

Declaration

In practice, this difference may become blurry as you can call a function and just ignore the return value, and, as a matter of fact, you can call a procedure and modify a value, a behavior which is caused by a function.

A procedure is declared with the `procedure` keyword and a function with the `function` keyword followed by the name you give. The name follows all the standard conventions in Delphi.

Procedures and functions that appear in the interface section in a unit are accessible in units that refer to this particular one. The `implementation` section holds the actual code for those procedures and functions. Procedures and functions can also be declared and implemented only in

J. Kouraklis, *Delphi Quick Syntax Reference*, https://doi.org/10.1007/978-1-4842-6112-5_4

the `implementation` section, but they are only accessible in this particular unit. In all other cases where you add code directly to the project file (e.g., console applications), the declarations and the code come together.

You can declare a procedure like this:

```
procedure simpleProc;
begin
  Writeln('This is the simplest procedure ever');
end;
```

Then, you invoke it by simply referring to its name as in the following code snippet:

```
begin
  simpleProc;
end.
```

A function is declared in a similar way, but you need to define the data type it returns:

```
function isNetworkAvailable: Boolean;
begin
  // Use some code to determine if network is available
  Result:=true; // or false
end;
```

In this example, the function returns a Boolean type (`true` or `false`). Delphi declares `result`, a very specific variable to capture the return value from a function. Every function should modify `result`; otherwise, the return value is undefined and may lead to unexpected effects in more complex code base. The result of the function can be assigned in a variable or can be used anywhere the specific return data type is needed as in the following `if` statement:

```
var
  netExists: Boolean;
begin
  netExists:=isNetworkAvailable;
  if isNetworkAvailable then
    Writeln('Network is available')
  else
    Writeln('There is no network available');
end.
```

As mentioned elsewhere, you can call a function without caring about the return value; just use the name to invoke it. This is a perfectly valid statement in Delphi, but the compiler issues a warning to let you know.

Parameters

The idea of routines in programming is that there is code that can be reused under different conditions because the algorithm that it implements is the same. The conditions are passed to routines in the form of parameters (or arguments as they are often called) and, in Delphi, they are enclosed in parentheses right after the name of the routine. As it can be seen in the previous examples, parameters are not necessary to declare routines. The next lines declare a procedure and function with parameters:

```
procedure updateLogs(logMessage: string);
begin
  // Normally you have some more sophisticated log container
  // This simple implementation is for demonstration
  Writeln(logMessage);
end;

function getLanguage(country: string): string;
begin
```

```
  if country = 'UK' then
    Result:='English';
end;
```

When a method takes more than one parameter, you declare them one after the other separated by a semicolon (;) as in the following cases:

```
procedure updateLogs(logMessage: string; logType: TLogType);
function getLanguage(country: string; showMostUsed: boolean):
string;
```

If your adjacent parameters are of the same type, then Delphi offers a less verbose way to declare them; you can separate them with a comma (,) before you declare the data type. The following declarations are equivalent:

```
procedure updateLogs(logMessage: string; logPrefix: string;
logType: TLogType);
procedure updateLogs(logMessage, logPrefix: string; logType:
TLogType);
```

The way to call them is exactly the same:

```
updateLogs('Image is not found', 'WARN', ltWarning);
```

The order of the parameters is important in terms of the data type they declare and must be followed when you call the methods. For updateLogs, the first parameter you pass must be of string value and the second of TLogType, whereas for getLanguage, the first must be a string and the second boolean.

```
updateLogs('There is an error', ltError);
Writeln(getLanguage('UK', true));
```

As we have already seen, parameter-less methods can be invoked by simply using their names. In Delphi, you can include a set of empty parentheses; in practice, it does not make any difference, and it is a convention to omit them.

```
simpleProc;
simpleProc(); // Equivalent calls
```

The Nature of Parameters

By now, we have recognized the need to declare the data type of the parameters. In Delphi, you can tweak the nature of the parameters in terms of how the compiler passes them from the point a method is called to the method itself. There are a number of options as discussed in the following sections.

Classic Parameters

The most typical and classic (default) way to pass parameters is just to declare the name and the data type. This is what we have done so far. In this instance, the compiler passes the parameters by value, which means that a copy of the value is passed to the method. Consider the following example:

```
procedure add100Classic(value: integer);
begin
  value:=value + 100;
  Writeln('The value in the procedure is ', value);
end;

var
  value: integer;
begin
  value:=100;
```

59

```
add100Classic(value);
Writeln('The value in the main block is ', value);
end.
```

This code shows that the value is 200 in the procedure, but it reverts back to 100 outside it. This is because the compiler passes a copy of value to add100, and therefore the addition of 100 affects the variable only within the context of the procedure. This is also a good example of the scope of a variable.

Constant Parameters

Prefixing the declaration of a parameter with the keyword const tells the compiler that the parameter is not to be altered inside the method. It behaves like a local constant. This means that the following code does not compile:

```
procedure add100Const(const value: integer);
begin
    value:=value + 100; // This does not compile
    Writeln('The value in the procedure is ', value);
end;
```

This is the rule but there are some exceptions. If the parameter is an object or a dynamic array, then const doesn't stop you from being able to modify the parameter. This has to do with the way the different compilers pass the parameters. In general, it is advisable to use const with parameters for two reasons: first, the compiler optimizes the generated code, and second, it prevents you from mistakenly modifying values when you should not.

Variable Parameters

When you pass a parameter to a method with the var prefix, the method can change the value of the parameter.

```
procedure add100Var(var value: integer);
begin
  value:=value + 100;
  Writeln('The value in the procedure is ', value);
end;
```

Now, the same code as in the classic approach shows that the value parameter is modified within add100Var.

Out Parameters

The only difference between var and out is that the latter simply tells the compiler to ignore any previous values of the parameter and clear it out. Then, it proceeds with any modifications that take place in the method.

```
procedure add100ToString(out value: string);
begin
  value:=value + '100';
  Writeln('Out: The value in the procedure is ', value);
end;

var
  valueStr: string;
begin
  valueStr:='300';
  Writeln('Out: The value  in the main block before the
  procedure is ', valueStr);
  add100ToString(valueStr);
  Writeln('Out: The value in the main block is ', valueStr);
end.
```

In this case, add100ToString ignores the value valueStr has when it enters the procedure and assumes it is an empty string. Then, it just adds the 100 string, which is what the main block accessed at the return point of the procedure.

There is more to the out parameters depending on the type of data the procedure expects, but it goes beyond the scope of this book. You can find more in the official documentation (Embarcadero, 2016).

The cases of var and out show that the boundaries between functions and procedures can get blurry. Normally, you would expect to use a function to return a modified value which is then consumed in the code, but now even procedures can provide variables that are altered within them. Equally, you can have functions that modify variables using var and out in their parameter list and, yet, return one more value as they normally do. This opens the possibility to construct functions that return more than one value.

Default Values of Parameters

Every parameter of every type and nature can have a default value (with a few exceptions) flagging the parameter as optional. You define default values by using the assignment symbol (=) within the parameter declaration as in the following example:

```
function addValue(const Value: integer; const Increment:
integer = 100): Integer;
begin
  result:=Value + Increment;
end;
```

```
begin
  Writeln('Default increment of 100 to 200: ',
                              addValue(200));
  Writeln('Custom increment of 500 to 200: ',
                              addValue(200, 500));
end.
```

If more than one optional parameter is declared, access to subsequent parameters requires you to add values to earlier parameters despite the existence of default values. This means you cannot skip parameters with default values when you call a procedure or a function. Suppose we declare the following function:

```
function moreThanOneDefault(const Value: integer;
                          const Iterations: Integer = 3;
                          const Increment: integer = 100):
                                                integer;
var
  num: Integer;
begin
  Result:=Value;
  for num := 1 to Iterations do
    Result:=result + Increment;
end;
```

The idea is that there are default values for the Iterations and the Increment step. If I want to pass a different increment step than the default, I need to provide a value for the Iterations parameter; I cannot simply skip it.

```
Writeln('Default increment of 100 for 3 iterations: ',
                      moreThanOneDefault(0));
Writeln('Custom increment of 500 for default iterations: ',
                    moreThanOneDefault(0, 3, 500));
```

Interrupting the Normal Execution

As suggested in the previous chapter, a call to Exit at any stage in a procedure or a function interrupts the normal execution of the method, and the code returns to the point of call of the method. The use of Exit is exactly the same as we have already seen in the previous chapter.

If Exit is called in a function, a parameter that matches the return type of the function can be passed as in the following example. If the function is declared as

```
function exitFunc: string;
```

then exiting and passing a result value can take place in the following form of Exit:

```
function exitFunc: string;
begin
  Exit('Just Exited the Function');
end;
```

Nested Methods

Procedures and functions can be declared (nested) within other procedures or functions. This is a situation we encounter often in recursive algorithms. Nested methods can be useful in a number of occasions.

The declaration follows the same rules, but they need to be declared and defined before the main begin..end block of the host method. Then, they can be called normally. Note that they are relevant and recognizable only within the scope of the host method.

As an example, the following procedure calculates the average of integers using a nested function:

```
function calculateAverage(const Values: array of Integer):
                                               double;
  function calculateSum: Integer;
  var
    num: Integer;
  begin
    Result:=0;
    for num := 0 to Length(Values) - 1 do
      Result:=Result + Values[num];
  end;
begin
  if Length(Values) > 1 then
    result:=calculateSum / Length(Values)
  else
    Result:=0.00;
end;
```

calculateSum is declared inside the host function. Note that the nested function can still access parameters and variables that belong to the host function. Because of this, there is an argument among developers that suggests nested functions slow down the execution of the code and they should be avoided.

Typed Methods

Typed method is a way to assign procedures or functions to a variable. In reality, what is being assigned is a pointer to the methods. This is why they are, often, called procedural pointers. From that point onward, the variable can be used to access and invoke the methods. The advantage of such approach is that the actual method can be changed on the spot and at runtime as long as declared conventions are followed. This allows Delphi code to implement callback functions.

To demonstrate the use of typed methods, let's assume we want to calculate the tax on income for two countries: the UK and Italy. The tax bands and the tax rates are different. First, we declare the blueprint of the tax function we are going to implement for each country. You can find the code in the TypedMethods unit in the code that comes with the book.

```
type
  TTaxFunc = function (const Amount: Double): Double;
```

This declaration indicates what our tax functions for each country should look like. In accordance to this line, we implement the two tax functions. For simplicity, I do not include the full code here, just the snippets to give you an idea that the algorithms are different. Note that the income bands and the tax rates are all fictitious.

```
function taxUK(const Amount: Double): Double;
begin
  Result:=0.00;
  if CompareValue(Amount, 10001) = LessThanValue then
    // Calculations; see source code
  else
    if CompareValue(Amount, 50001) = LessThanValue  then
    begin
      // Calculations; see source code
    end
    else
    begin
      // Calculations; see source code
    end;
end;
```

```
function taxItaly(const Amount: Double): Double;
begin
  Result:=0.00;
  if CompareValue(Amount, 100001) = LessThanValue   then
  begin
    // Calculations; see source code
  end
  else
  begin
    // Calculations; see source code
  end;
end;
```

We access the two functions via a variable of TTaxFunc type:

```
var
  taxFunc: TTaxFunc;
```

Once we have the variable, we can assign and, consequently, invoke the correct function as in the code that follows:

```
begin
  taxFunc:=taxUK;
  Writeln('For UK: ', taxFunc(80000));
  taxFunc:=taxItaly;
  Writeln('For Italy: ', taxFunc(80000));
end.
```

In this example, TTaxFunc receives parameters. In the case of parameter-less functions and procedures, nothing changes. You invoke them simply by referring to their names. In the example code of this book, check the showMenu procedure.

Anonymous Methods

Anonymous method is a technique that allows a block of code (the body of the method) to be passed to a variable without the need to explicitly declare and name a method. There are many benefits from an approach like this; methods are declared only when they are needed, dynamic change of methods can occur, and more extensible code can evolve.

The declaration of an anonymous method follows the same pattern as in the case of typed methods with the addition of the keyword reference.

```
type
  TAnonProc = reference to procedure;
  TAnonFunc = reference to function (const switch: string):
  string;
```

Then, in the code, a procedure or a function is assigned to a variable, and the method is invoked by directly referring to the variable as in the following example:

```
var
  proc: TAnonProc;
begin
  proc:=procedure
        begin
          Writeln('A call from inside an anonymous procedure');
        end;
  proc;
end.
```

The approach allows access to variables that do not belong to the anonymous method but are available in the same scope where the method exists (variable binding). In other words, if I declare a variable in the main begin..end block in the preceding code, I can access it in the begin..end block of the anonymous method. Consider the following anonymous function. It is able to capture the temperature variable although it is not part of the function.

```
var
  func: TAnonFunc;
  temperature: integer;
begin
  func:= function(const switch: string): string
         begin
           Write('The temperature is '+temperature.ToString+'
           and the heating is '+switch+'. ');
           if temperature <= 24 then
           begin
             if switch='ON' then
               writeln('The room will get warm soon');
             if switch='OFF' then
               writeln('Maybe you need to turn the heating on?');
           end
           else
           begin
             if switch='ON' then
               writeln('This may be getting very hot...');
             if switch='OFF' then
               writeln('Nice...you save energy and help the
               environment');
           end;
         end;

  Randomize;
  for temperature := 16 to 28 do
  begin
    if Random(100) < 50 then
      func('ON')
    else
```

```
    func('OFF');
  end;
end.
```

Lastly, since anonymous methods start with a type declaration, they can very well serve as parameters in other methods increasing their flexibility.

```
procedure anonFuncWithParam(const func: TAnonFunc);
begin
  func('INTERMEDIATE SWITCH STATE');
end;
```

Here we define anonFuncWithParam which accepts an anonymous function of TAnonFunc type as a parameter. Then, it simply invokes func with a hard-coded string.

We can pass a TAnonFunc to the procedure either by declaring a variable first and then passing it as a parameter or, more directly, by writing the function code right at the place of the parameter.

```
begin
  anonFuncWithParam(function (const switch: string): string
                    begin
                      Writeln('The current swith state is:
                                            '+switch);
                    end);
end.
```

In this implementation, note that we do not need to add a semicolon (;) after the declaration of the function and after the final end as we would expect if we had a normal function defined.

In the code we developed in this section, we declared our own typed method (TAnonFunc). Delphi provides a set of predefined methods already available to developers. You will find them in System.SysUtils unit, and they are generic; this means that we can define the actual type of variables they can handle in parameters and the result type.

```
type
  ...
  TFunc<T,TResult> = reference to function (Arg1: T):
                                                    TResult;
```

Therefore, in the preceding examples, we could declare func by simply writing this line:

```
var
  func: TFunc<string, string>;
```

Note that Arg1 in the definition of TFunc is not declared as constant parameter. If we use this approach, we need to remove the keyword const when we assign the actual function to the func variable.

This is a quick introduction to the way anonymous methods work. You can find more information in the official documentation (Embarcadero, 2016) and have a look at Nick Hodges's book (Hodges, 2014).

Method Overloading

Overloading a method means that you can declare two or more methods with the same name but different parameter list or, in the case of functions, different return types. The *difference* can be either in the number of the parameters or the type of the parameters. In Delphi, we use the keyword overload to declare such methods.

```
procedure multiProc; overload;
procedure multiProc(const Value: string); overload;
procedure multiProc(const Value: string; const SubElement:
integer); overload;
```

When the procedure is invoked, the compiler determines which version should be called by scanning through the declarations and matching the number and the types of the parameters. These are the only two criteria the compiler uses for this purpose. Consequently, overloading cannot work for parameters of different nature (e.g., const and var).

```
procedure multiProc(const Value: string); overload;
// This overloading approach does not work
procedure multiProc(var Value: string); overload;
```

Summary

In this chapter, we looked at how procedures and functions work in Delphi. We differentiated between them, discussed the different types of parameters they can manage, and visited different ways to use them in the code.

References

Embarcadero, 2016. *Anonymous Methods in Delphi.* [Online] Available at: http://docwiki.embarcadero.com/RADStudio/Sydeny/en/Anonymous_Methods_in_Delphi [Accessed 03 06 2020].

Embarcadero, 2016. *Parameters (Delphi).* [Online] Available at: http://docwiki.embarcadero.com/RADStudio/Sydeny/en/Parameters_(Delphi)#Out_Parameters [Accessed 03 06 2020].

Hodges, N., 2014. *Coding in Delphi.* s.l.:Nepeta Enterprises.

CHAPTER 5

Object-Oriented Programming (OOP)

Delphi supports full object-oriented programming (OOP). In OOP, the most fundamental entity is an object. An object is characterized by its state (implemented by data) and what sort of capabilities it has (functionality). For example, a computer can be described as an object in a particular state (e.g., available memory, screen resolution, computational power, etc.) being able to provide several functions (e.g., connect to the Internet, edit a text file, convert an image, etc.). In the rest of the chapter, we look at the fundamentals of OOP in Delphi.

Declaration

The theoretical concept in OOP of an object is implemented in Delphi (as in most of the languages) by declaring a class and an instance of the class. This instance is the object and is accessed via a variable. The following lines define a class and an object:

```
type
  TComputer = class

  end;
var
  myComputer: TComputer;
```

© John Kouraklis 2020
J. Kouraklis, *Delphi Quick Syntax Reference*, https://doi.org/10.1007/978-1-4842-6112-5_5

You can declare a class in either the `interface` or `implementation` section of a unit. The difference is that if it appears in the latter, the class is only available to the unit, whereas a declaration in `interface` makes the class available anywhere the unit appears in the `uses` clause. You can also declare a class within another class to serve your coding needs.

The variable provides access to the class, but we are not ready to use it yet. We first need to create an instance of the class (an object) by calling `Create`. Note that this is the most fundamental way to instantiate an object. `Create` does a couple of things behind the scene with the most important being that it allocates memory for the object. When we finish with the object, we need to make this memory available for other objects and applications. In Delphi, we do this by calling `Free`. The following code snippet demonstrates a typical flow when we deal with objects:

```
begin
  myComputer:=TComputer.Create;
  // use myComputer here
  myComputer.Free;
end.
```

If you use Delphi 10.3 and above, you can take advantage of the inline variables and declare the variable and instantiate the object in one line.

```
begin
  // This works only in 10.3 and above
  var myComputer:=TComputer.Create;
  // use myComputer here
  myComputer.Free;
end.
```

If you try to access the state and functionality of an object without first calling `Create`, the application will crash by generating an access violation exception. If you forget to call `Free`, the application will continue working perfectly fine, but the memory chunk that was reserved for the object will not be released, and therefore memory leaks will occur.

When you declare an object (but before you instantiate), it is not yet initialized. Recent versions of Delphi signify this by setting the reference variable to nil. It is easy to check the state of an object using the Assigned function.

```
if Assigned(myComputer) then
  ...
```

Assigned returns True if myComputer has been instantiated. As mentioned earlier, only recent versions set the objects to nil. In older ones, the state of objects is undetermined until Create is called.

Object State (Fields)

The state of an object is held internally in fields and properties. In Delphi, a field and a property can be of any data type or of other classes. In this next line, we declare a field:

```
type
  TComputer = class
    Memory: Word;
  end;
```

We, then, access the field using the dot notation:

```
myComputer.Memory:=32;
```

One of the cornerstone ideas in OOP is that when objects are used in code, the fields and the properties (class members) are not always accessible (encapsulation). This depends on the visibility level of the fields and the properties.

In Delphi, there are four levels of visibility growing from the very restrictive private members to openly accessible public and published members:

- private: Accessible only to the class.

- protected: Accessible only to descendent classes (more on this in the section "Inheritance").

- public: Accessible to any instance of the class.

- published: Same as public with additional compiler information and ability to show them in the form designer. Note that not all data types can be publishable.

There are more levels of visibility (e.g., strict, automated, etc.), but they serve more specific requirements. The declaration of members with different visibility can be done in any order you see relevant, but best coding practice suggests that fields and properties appear in the class in the order of less restrictive to least restrictive visibility.

```
type
  TComputerBuild = class
  private
    fDisplayedMemory: string;
  protected

  public
    Memory: Word;
  published

  end;
```

As mentioned elsewhere, the fields can be of other class types. This implies that this class type must be defined before referenced. In most of the cases, you will be able to maintain an order in the declarations to meet this requirement. On the downside, this creates a form of dependency which may not be needed or may be impossible to keep in mutually dependent classes as in the following example:

```
type
  TComputerBuild = class
  private
    ...
  protected
    ...
  public
    HardDrive: THardDrive;
    ...
  published
    ...
  end;

  THardDrive = class
  public
    Capacity: Word;
    HostComputer: TComputerBuild;
  end;
```

The preceding code will not compile because THardDrive is referenced before declared. Moving the declaration before TComputerBuild poses the same problem. The way to deal with this situation is to forward declare a class, that is, to provide the name but defer the full declaration. This is done by adding this line right after the type keyword:

```
type
  THardDrive = class;
  TComputerBuild = class
    ...
  end;
```

Object Functionality (Methods)

The functionality (or capabilities) of an object is revealed by class methods; that is, procedures and functions that serve the purpose and scope of the object. The declarations follow the typical procedure and function semantics we visited in previous chapters. As an example, let's introduce methods to shut down our computer (class):

```
type
  TComputerBuild = class
    ...
  public
    ...
    procedure shutDown;
  published
    ...
  end;
```

shutdown is a publicly available method, and it is implemented under the name TComputerBuild.shutDown. In the IDE, you can type in the full procedure declaration, or you can click somewhere inside the class and press Ctrl-Shift-C. RAD Studio will create the blueprint for you.

```
procedure TComputerBuild.shutDown;
begin
  // Now shut the computer down
end;
```

Methods in classes can have different levels of accessibility in the same way fields and properties do. In the code that follows, killAllPrograms is a private method and can only be called from inside the class. If you try to access it outside the class, the code will not compile.

```
type
  TComputerBuild = class
  private

    ...

    procedure killAllPrograms;
  public

    ...

  published

    ...

  end;

procedure TComputerBuild.killAllPrograms;
begin

  ...

end;

procedure TComputerBuild.shutDown;
begin
  killAllPrograms;

  ...

end;
```

We access the methods in the class using the dot notation which is what we did when we wanted to access the class fields.

```
var
  buildComputer: TComputerBuild;
begin
  buildComputer:=TComputerBuild.Create;
  // This does not compile
//  buildComputer.killAllPrograms;
  buildComputer.shutDown;
  buildComputer.Free;
end.
```

Overloading of procedures and functions works in classes as well. In theory, you can have overloaded methods with any visibility, but in OOP context, it usually makes sense with protected and public methods.

```
type
  TComputerBuild = class
    ...
  public
    ...
    procedure add(const aUser: string); overload;
    procedure add(const aHD: THardDrive); overload;
  end;
```

We have already discussed how we create a new instance of an object and destroy it. The constructor (Create) and the destructor (Destroy) are special methods for objects as they run a lot of initialization and finalization code for objects. Constructors can be overloaded to allow developers to add their own initialization code. But there is a small twist in Delphi; you cannot use the same name for the overloaded constructor (Create). In the following example, we introduce a new constructor (CreateWithHD) that receives a THardDrive class in a typical dependency injection fashion.

```
type
  TComputerBuild = class
    ...
  public
    constructor CreateWithHD(const aHardDrive: THardDrive);
    ...
  end;
```

```
constructor TComputerBuild.Create(const aHardDrive:
THardDrive);
begin
  inherited Create;
  // Add more initialisation code here
end;
```

There are three points worth mentioning: firstly, there is a specific order to declare fields and methods within a visibility block; fields appear first with methods following. Otherwise, the code does not compile.

Secondly, a constructor in classes is defined with the `constructor` keyword, and, lastly, it is very important to call the default constructor using the statement `inherited Create` inside the new one. This will allow the object to be initialized correctly.

Destructors in Delphi, as in every programming language, cannot be overloaded. When we want to execute code before the object is destroyed, we *override* the destructor using the `override` keyword. The last call should always be `inherited` or `inherited Destroy`.

```
type
  TComputerBuild = class
    ...
  Public
    destructor Destroy; override;
    ...
  end;

destructor TComputerBuild.Destroy;
begin
  // Add code here
  inherited;
end;
```

Object State (Properties)

In the previous section, we saw how fields can be used to store the state of an object. Although they are sufficient for this purpose, fields are limited in scope as they purely work as data storage.

Delphi extends the idea of fields and offers properties—a field-like declaration with the ability to manipulate the stored data. Properties, as all other class elements, can be managed in terms of visibility and accessibility by following the private, protected, public, and published grouping. A property that resembles fields is declared as follows:

```
type
  THardDrive = class
  private
    ...
  public
    ...
    property Manufacturer: string read fManufacturer write
    fManufacturer;
  end;
```

Properties can do much more than simply refer to a field. As seen in the preceding code line, each property has a setter (`write`) and a getter (`read`) part which can be a field (as shown here) or a method. If the setter is omitted, then the property is read-only, and if the getter is omitted, the property is considered as write-only.

In the case of a method, the setter is a procedure with one parameter of the same data type as the property, and the getter is a function that returns an item of the same data type as the property.

```
type
  THardDrive = class
  private
    ...
```

```
    fSerial: string;
    function getSerial: String;
    procedure setSerial(const Value: String);
  public

    ...

    property Serial: String read getSerial write setSerial;
  end;

function THardDrive.getSerial: String;
begin
  result:=fSerial;
end;

procedure THardDrive.setSerial(const Value: String);
begin
  fSerial:=Value.ToLower;
end;
```

Serial property sets the value of a holder field (fSerial) via
setSerial and returns the value of the field via getSerial. The ability to
use setter and getter methods for properties allows for ad hoc modification
of the value of the properties. In the following code, we create a new
instance of THardDrive and pass the serial in block capital:

```
var
  hardDrive: THardDrive;
begin
  hardDrive:=THardDrive.Create;
  hardDrive.Serial:='XHHJU-56748-ABC';
  Writeln(hardDrive.Serial);
  hardDrive.Free;
end.
```

The call to assign the string to the Serial property passes the value to
fSerial field after it converts the string to lowercase (ToLower). Then, the
writeln statement retrieves the value by triggering getSerial.

Properties do not have to be monodimensional. They can handle
declarations that look like an array (array properties). For example, let's
introduce property Content in THardDrive that gives access to the byte of a
specific cylinder and sector.

```
type
  THardDrive = class
  private
    ...
    fContent: array[0..1000, 0..10000] of Byte;
    function getContent(Cylinder, Sector: Word): byte;
    procedure setContent(Cylinder, Sector: Word; const Value:
    byte);
  public
    ...
    property Content[Cylinder, Sector: Word]: byte read
    getContent write setContent;
  end;

function THardDrive.getContent(Cylinder, Sector: Word): byte;
begin
  // Note that there is no check of boundary values for
     fContent
  Result:=fContent[Cylinder, Sector];
end;

procedure THardDrive.setContent(Cylinder, Sector: Word; const
Value: byte);
begin
```

```
// Note that there is no check of boundary values for
    fContent
fContent[Cylinder, Sector]:=Value;
end;
```

The logic behind the setter and getter is the same as in the case of a simple property. Note that array properties cannot be mapped directly to a field, and thus the use of a getter and setter is compulsory. Although the examples here and in most of other textbooks and articles show that a property declaration goes together with a local and private field, this is not necessary. In more complex implementations and in different scenarios, the getter method may access a dataset to retrieve database entries, and a setter may use a cloud storage to pass the value of a property.

The only step that is left is to provide some initial values to fContent. We can simply use the constructor for this purpose.

```
type
THardDrive = class
public
    constructor Create;
    ...
end;
constructor THardDrive.Create;
var
    cyl: Integer;
    sec: integer;
begin
    inherited;
    Randomize;
    for cyl := Low(fContent) to High(fContent) do
        for sec := Low(fContent[cyl]) to High(fContent[cyl]) do
            fContent[cyl, sec]:=Random(255);
end;
```

Then, accessing the content of THardDrive is a matter of a simple call as follows:

```
writeln(hardDrive.Content[100, 100]);
```

Published properties are, fundamentally, public properties with added runtime compiler information. In graphical applications and especially in code that supports graphical components, published properties are used by Delphi IDE to provide design-time properties and events. For the interested reader who wants to dive into the world of component writing, Delphi Component Writer's Guide (Anon., n.d) and Thorpe's book (1996) on the subject provide very good insight on the topic.

Class Members and Methods

The typical use of objects indicates the instantiation of an object via a call to a constructor and, when the object is not needed anymore, a call to destructor in order to free up the reserved memory, as we have already seen.

In Delphi, we can introduce fields, properties, and methods that can be accessible without the need to follow this memory management cycle. They are declared using the class keyword, and they can be helpful in cases where a property or a field needs to hold a value among different instances of an object. Class methods give the option to organize methods in classes but without the need to create and destroy them all the time.

To demonstrate the concept, the following code declares a class to represent a custom application and defines a class property to hold the operating systems the application supports.

```
type
  TOSList = array[0..2] of string;
  TCustomApplication = class
  private
```

```
  class function getSupportedOS: TOSList; static;
public
  class property SupportedOS: TOSList read getSupportedOS;
end;
```

SupportedOS is a read-only property which uses a function (getSupportedOS) to populate itself.

```
class function TCustomApplication.getSupportedOS: TOSList;
begin
  Result[0]:='Windows 7';
  Result[1]:='Windows 8';
  Result[2]:='Windows 10';
end;
```

As mentioned already, a class property needs the class keyword. The same is required for the getter and setter methods of the property. Moreover, these methods need to be static as can be seen in the preceding code. Now, we do not need to create the class object or destroy it; a simple call to the property will work perfectly.

```
var
  os: string;
begin
  for os in TCustomApplication.SupportedOS do
    Writeln(os);
end.
```

Inheritance

Inheritance in OOP is an implementation feature that allows new classes (subclasses or child classes) to be defined based on already defined classes that act as base (parent or super) classes. The importance of inheritance comes from the fact that this approach allows shared state (properties) and functionality (methods) among the parent and child classes. Moreover, inherited classes are able to modify the shared properties and methods making them extensible.

We have already defined TCustomApplication. This time we want to derive classes that represent different types of applications based on this class. The derived classes will have a property called AppType to indicate the application type (financial, game, utility). AppType's data type is TApplicationType. First, let's define a base class for our applications that extends TCustomApplication.

```
type
  TApplicationType = (atUndefined, atFinancial, atGame, atUtility);
  TBaseApplication = class (TCustomApplication)
  private
    fAppType: TApplicationType;
  public
    property AppType: TApplicationType read fAppType write fAppType;
  end;
```

Nothing new here apart from the first line of the class definition which says that TBaseApplication is a subclass of (or inherits from) TCustomApplication.

TBaseApplication needs to initialize the application type to atUndefined. The most natural place to do this is in the constructor of the class. This time, though, we want the subclasses to be able to modify this value. In order to achieve this, we need to declare the constructor as virtual. This tells the compiler that the constructor can be modified in inherited classes.

```
type
  TBaseApplication = class (TCustomApplication)
  public
    constructor Create; virtual;

    ...
  end;
```

In this case, we set the application type to atUndefined. Note in the following code that we first call inherited before we do anything else in the constructor.

```
constructor TBaseApplication.Create;
begin
  inherited;
  fAppType:=atUndefined;
end;
```

In terms of how we access AppType property, we follow the same pattern: we declare a variable, create an instance of the object, and process the property.

```
var
  app: TBaseApplication;
begin
  app:=TBaseApplication.Create;
  // Access the property with app.AppType
  app.Free;
end.
```

Let's create a new financial application by subclassing TBaseApplication as there is no limit to how many subclasses you can have.

```
type
  TFinApplication = class (TBaseApplication)
  public
    constructor Create; override;
  end;
```

TFinApplication inherits from TBaseApplication. This means that the new class has the AppType property, which we need to modify. In order to do this, we override the constructor using the override keyword.

```
constructor TFinApplication.Create;
begin
  inherited;
  fAppType:=atFinancial;
end;
```

One more time, the call to inherited is the first step. This will make the compiler go back to the inheritance tree and invoke the initial constructor. This is done with all the base classes.

Managing TFinApplication as an object is simple, and it is done by declaring a variable of TFinApplication. Additionally, another concept from OOP (polymorphism) allows us to use TFinApplication where TBaseApplication is expected. Therefore, the following code is valid:

```
var
  app: TBaseApplication;
begin
  app:=TFinApplication.Create;
  ...
  app.Free;
end.
```

Overriding methods also works when methods have different levels of visibility. Our applications, surely, have version numbers. We can add a relevant property (Version) to TBaseApplication which defines the getter method to be virtual and protected. This means that the method can be overridden by ancestors but only by them as indicated by the protected nature of it.

```
type
  TBaseApplication = class (TCustomApplication)
  private

    ...

  protected
    function getVersion: string; virtual;
  public

    ...

    property Version: string read getVersion;
  end;

function TBaseApplication.getVersion: string;
begin
  Result := '0.0.0';
end;
```

TFinApplication can now override getVersion to declare its own version status.

```
type
  TFinApplication = class (TBaseApplication)
  protected
    function getVersion: string; override;
  public

    ...

  end;
```

```
function TFinApplication.getVersion: string;
begin
  Result:='3.2.2-alpha';
end;
```

The following code demonstrates which getVersion functions are called. In the first call, the TBaseApplication function is invoked, and in the second, the inherited one as defined by TFinApplication.

```
var
  app: TBaseApplication;
begin
  app:=TBaseApplication.Create;
  Writeln(app.Version); // Prints 0.0.0
  app.Free;

  app:=TFinApplication.Create;
  Writeln(app.Version); // Prints 3.2.2-alpha
  app.Free;
end.
```

You may, now, wonder how we can differentiate which class is assigned to app. In this example, the two classes are the same (TBaseApplication, TFinApplication) but, in general, we create descendants because we want to add additional extensions. Let's go ahead and create a game application (TGameApplication). This class has one more property called MultiPlayer of Boolean type. I omit the constructor here, which initializes the property as it is not important at this stage. You can see the full implementation in the code file that accompanies this book.

```
type
  TGameApplication = class (TBaseApplication)
  private
    fMultiPlayer: boolean;
```

```
public
  property MultiPlayer: boolean read fMultiPlayer write
  fMultiPlayer;
end;
```

Consistent to OOP principles, we can create a TGameApplication using the app variable. This time we want to check if the game is multiplayer or not, but the app is basically a TBaseApplication variable.

TBaseApplication does not have the MultiPlayer property, but TGameApplication does. Thus, we need to check whether the app is of TGameApplication type. We do this using the is operator. Once we are certain we have the correct class, we can use the as operator to access the MultiPlayer variable. This method of enforcing the compiler to treat a specific variable as of specific type is called type casting.

```
begin
  ...
  if app is TGameApplication then
    writeln('MultiPlayer: ',
                    (app as TGameApplication).MultiPlayer);
  ...
end.
```

Interfaces

Class inheritance is fundamental to extending a class and adding new functionality. In recent years, the OOP landscape is moving toward writing classes that are more decoupled between each other. This leads to more flexibility and higher level of abstraction.

In Delphi and, as a matter of fact, in almost all OOP languages, abstraction is achieved by defining interfaces (or object interfaces). An interface can indicate the state of the class (properties and fields) and what the class can do (methods). The important message here is that implementation details are separated from the manifest that indicates the properties and methods of a class. For example, in the case of password generation, there are quite many encryption algorithms in use. Interfaces allow us to switch to alternative implementations. The following snippet defines IPasswordGenerator and IPassword interfaces:

```
type
  TPasswordAlgorithm = (paAES, paSHA);
  IPasswordGenerator = interface
    ['{16C5CD04-5051-4557-BA3C-3AE932147C6A}']

    function getAlgorithm: TPasswordAlgorithm;
    function encrypt (const aValue: string): string;

    property Algorithm: TPasswordAlgorithm read getAlgorithm;
  end;

  IPassword = interface
    ['{6C85FF1F-C5BC-4E66-974D-1622A6F908A7}']
    function encryptPassword (const aPassword: string): string;
  end;
```

It is customary, but not enforced by Delphi, to use the letter 'I' at the beginning of the name of an interface. What is important though is that each interface requires a unique number (GUID)*—again, not enforced by Delphi, but it saves from a lot of troubles in complex code base. You can see the GUIDs enclosed in the square brackets in the preceding examples. You can use your own GUIDs, but they need to adhere to the letter grouping shown in the preceding code. If you are in Delphi IDE, hitting Ctrl-Shift-G will add one for you. The preceding code also demonstrates that we can use both properties and methods in interfaces.

---

*There is one exception to this; the consensus among Delphi developers is that interfaces with generics better not be given a GUID.

We, now, need to add the implementation classes. We create two classes that implement the two different algorithms as indicated by TPasswordAlgorithm. When classes implement interfaces, they should derive from an interface supporting class with TInterfacedObject being the most common:

```
type
  TAESAlgorithm = class (TInterfacedObject, IPasswordGenerator)
  private
    fAlgorithm: TPasswordAlgorithm;
  public
    constructor Create;
    function encrypt (const aValue: string): string;
    function getAlgorithm: TPasswordAlgorithm;
  end;

constructor TAESAlgorithm.Create;
begin
  inherited;
  fAlgorithm:=paAES;
end;

function TAESAlgorithm.encrypt(const aValue: string): string;
begin
  // use AES algorithm
  Result:=aValue+' - AES Encrypted';
end;

function TAESAlgorithm.getAlgorithm: TPasswordAlgorithm;
begin
  Result:=fAlgorithm;
end;
```

Classes that bind to interfaces must implement all the methods of an interface; otherwise, the code does not compile. Only what is described in the interface declaration is accessible from consumers of the class, and they all come with public visibility.

You can check whether a class implements an interface using the Supports function as in the next lines.

```
if Supports(password, IPassword) then
  Writeln('Interface is supported')
else
  Writeln('Interface is not supported');
```

Let's implement one more password algorithm. This time, the interface methods are declared as private in the class, but this has no actual effect. Since methods and properties are declared in an interface, they are all public.

```
type
  TSHAAlgorithm = class (TInterfacedObject, IPasswordGenerator)
  private
    fAlgorithm: TPasswordAlgorithm;
    function encrypt (const aValue: string): string;
    function getAlgorithm: TPasswordAlgorithm;
  public
    constructor Create;
  end;
```

Using interfaced classes is slightly different to using non-interfaced ones. Instead of declaring the variable to be of the class type, we declare it against the interface.

```
var
  generatorAES: IPasswordGenerator;
  generatorSHA: IPasswordGenerator;
```

```
  password: IPassword;
begin
  generatorAES:=TAESAlgorithm.Create;
  generatorSHA:=TSHAAlgorithm.Create;

  password:=TPassword.Create(generatorAES);
  writeln(password.encryptPassword('tywqeri'));

  password:=TPassword.Create(generatorSHA);
  Writeln(password.encryptPassword('435'));
end.
```

Then, they are instantiated using the (interfaced) classes and the typical call to Create. password instance shows how abstraction works; the constructor receives IPasswordGenerator as parameter which accepts any class that implements this particular interface. Therefore, we can supply any of the generators we wish.

The second point to raise is the difference in managing the life cycle of interfaces compared to objects. When we manage objects, we follow the pattern Create..Free in order to return any reserved memory to the system. With interfaces, this is done automatically as they are reference counted, and the compiler can release the reserved memory. Therefore, we do not call Free with interfaces as it will lead to compilation error.

Cross-Platform Memory Management

Developers are responsible to manage the memory of the objects, as we have already seen. The classic and standard way to do this is to follow the pattern we have seen a few times already.

```
var
  newObj: TMyClass;
begin
```

97

```
  newObj:=TMyClass.Create;
  // Use newObj
  newObj.Free;
end.
```

An object is instantiated by the constructor (Create), and the memory is released by a call to destructor (Free). In fact, this is not the complete pattern coders in Delphi use; it comes with a safety check in case of exceptions.

An exception is the error management model Delphi uses, and it is in contrast to models where errors are indicated by error codes. In the case where a runtime error occurs, Delphi will signal the whole application about this error by forcibly interrupting the execution of the application at the point where the error is detected. Developers in Delphi talk about this situation by saying that an exception has been raised (or thrown).

For example, if we try to access a database, all sort of things can go wrong that do not depend on the stability and quality of our code. Suppose we attempt to execute an SQL query and pass the results to a TMyClass object.

```
var
  newObj: TMyClass;
begin
  newObj:=TMyClass.Create;
  // Retrieve data from the database
  // This line executes the SQL query and raises exception
newObj.Free;
end.
```

If an exception occurs, the code will exit by skipping the call to Free. This means that newObj will never get the chance to release the memory it occupies. In this way, a classic memory leak will occur.

The proper way to deal with this situation is to wrap the execution code in a try..finally block.

```
begin
  newObj:=TMyClass.Create;
  try
    // Retrieve data from the database
    // This line executes the SQL query and raises exception
finally
    newObj.Free;
  end;
end.
```

This pattern guarantees that the code inside the finally branch is always executed regardless whether an exception is thrown or not.

The memory management model that was described earlier and indicated that the developer is responsible for the memory allocation of objects is called the Manual Reference Counting model. We have also seen a slightly different memory management model when interfaces are used. In this case, the developer does not need to *free* an interface manually because the compiler is able to automatically track the references on the object instances in memory and release them accordingly. If the compiler is able to do this, then it uses the Automatic Reference Counting (ARC) model.

The Delphi compilers for desktop applications (Windows 32-bit, Windows 64-bit, macOS 32-bit, macOS 64-bit, Linux 64-bit) do not use ARC for classes. In versions Delphi XE4 up until 10.3, the ARC model has been introduced for mobile platforms. This means that code without explicit calls to Free is perfectly suitable to manage objects; when the object instance goes out of scope, the compiler frees it automatically.

```
var
  newObj: TMyClass;
begin
  newObj:=TMyClass.Create;
  // Use newObj
  // We do not need to call newObj.Free
end.
```

According to the official documentation (Embarcadero, 2015), in the vast majority of the cases, the preceding approach is sufficient. There are some special scenarios where more need to be done to trigger the release of the object. This can be done with a call to DisposeOf method. DisposeOf can also be called in the classic compilers (Windows, macOS) without any harm, but the official recommendation is to use Free in desktop compilers and DisposeOf with mobile compilers.

In practical terms, writing cross-platform code that manages objects looks like the one in the following lines. The code takes advantage of a compile directive ({$IFDEF}..{$ENDIF}) to supply the correct code according to the compilation platform. For completeness, the code includes a call to try..finally which deals with exceptions.

```
var
  newObj: TMyClass;
begin
  newObj:=TMyClass.Create;
  try
    // Use newObj
  finally
    {$IFDEF AUTOREFCOUNT}
      newObj.DisposeOf;
    {$ELSE}
      newObj.Free;
```

```
  {$ENDIF}
 end;
end.
```

Starting from Delphi version 10.4, the ARC model for classes on mobile platforms has been deactivated, and the classic approach to managing the lifetime of objects is now the only way to instantiate and destroy objects (Cantu, 2018) that are not implemented via interfaces.

This is a short discussion on the topic of memory management on classic and mobile compilers. There is a wealth of sources to allow you to further your knowledge. I would recommend the book by Chris Rolliston (Rolliston, 2012). It comes in three parts and it is based on Delphi XE2, but it covers quite extensively a breadth of topics, and it includes a very good discussion on objects. The book that investigates the memory management models in Delphi to great extent and explores different coding approaches is written by Prasnikar and Prasnikar Jr. (Prasnikar & Prasnikar, 2017), and it is highly recommended.

Summary

In this chapter, we started object-oriented programming (OOP) from scratch. We saw how we declare classes and define objects. Then, we looked at how Delphi implements object states and functionality to deploy full OOP support. We covered interfaces—an abstract way to define functionality loosely coupled to implementation details. Lastly, we looked at ways to manage the life cycle of objects.

References

Anon., n.d. *Delphi Component Writer's Guide.* [Online] Available at: `https://doc.lagout.org/programmation/Delphi/Delphi/Delphi%20 -%20Delphi%20Component%20Writer's%20Guide-%20Delphi%20for%20 Windows.pdf` [Accessed 23 04 2020].

Cantu, M., 2018. *Directions for ARC Memory Management in Delphi.* [Online] Available at: `https://blog.marcocantu.com/blog/2018- october-Delphi-ARC-directions.html` [Accessed 24 04 2020].

Embarcadero, 2015. *Automatic Reference Counting in Delphi Mobile Compilers.* [Online] Available at: `http://docwiki.embarcadero.com/ RADStudio/Rio/en/Automatic_Reference_Counting_in_Delphi_Mobile_ Compilers` [Accessed 24 04 2020].

Prasnikar, D. & Prasnikar, N. J., 2017. *Delphi Memory Management: For Classic and ARC Compilers.* 1st Edition ed. s.l.:s.n.

Rolliston, C., 2012. *Delphi XE2 Foundations: Part 1.* s.l.:s.n.

Thorpe, D., 1996. *Delphi Component Design.* s.l.:s.n.

Index

A, B

Anonymous method, 68–70
Automatic Reference Counting
    (ARC) model, 99

C

Case statement, 32, 50–51
Comments, 41
Conditional statement
    case, 50
    definition, 48
    if, 48–49
Constants, 40
Custom managed records, 34

D, E

Data types
    arrays, 28–31
    boolean values, 22
    char, 21
    enumerated types, 22
    floating-point, 24
    generics, 37–39
    integer, 20
    pointers, 35, 36
    real, 23

records, 31–35
sets, 27, 28
strings, 25–27
subrange, 23
variant, 36, 37
Delphi Pascal
    definition, 1
    forms/frames, 6
    IDEs, 7, 8, 14
    multiple
        platforms, 3, 4
    naming conventions, 15
    native code, 3
    OOP language, 2
    project files, 4
    simplest application
        (console), 9–11
    simplest application
        (graphical), 11, 12, 14
    syntax, 1, 2
    units, 5, 6
    VCL, 3
DisposeOf method, 100

F

FireMonkey (FMX) framework, 3
For statement, 46

V

Variables
  age, 19
  definition, 17
  example, 18
  identifier, 17

scope, 19
Visual Component
    Library (VCL), 3

W, X, Y, Z

while..do statement, 43